New book releases are free the first 48 hours. Every month, there is a free download on Kindle. To know of new releases and dates for free downloads, please subscribe at

www.TessaCason.com

Tessa Cason
5694 Mission Ctr. Rd. #602-213
San Diego, CA. 92108
www.TessaCason.com
Tessa@TessaCason.com

© Tessa Cason, 2019.

All rights reserved. No part of this work may be reproduced, published, or transmitted electronically without express written permission from the publisher.

Copyright of all images used in this book belong to their respective owners.

LEGAL NOTICE AND DISCLAIMER:

From author and publisher: The information in this book is not intended to diagnose or treat any particular disease and/or condition. Nothing contained herein is meant to replace qualified medical or psychological advice and/or services. The author and publisher do not assume responsibility for how the reader chooses to apply the techniques herein. Use of the information is at the reader's discretion and discernment. The author and publisher specifically disclaim any and all liability arising directly or indirectly from the use or application contained in this book.

Nothing contained in this book is to be considered medical advice for any specific situation. This information is not intended as a substitute for the advice or medical care of a Physician prior to taking any personal action with respect to the information contained in this book. This book and all of its contents are intended for educational and informational purpose only. The information in this book is believed to be reliable, but is presented without guaranty or warranty.

By reading further, you agree to release the author and publisher from any damages or injury associated with your use of the material in this book.

300 EFT Tapping Statements™ for Intuition

Tessa Cason, MA

My Intuition Story

"Mom," I asked. "Why are Elaine and Doug getting a divorce?"

"How do you know they are getting a divorce? Are you listening on the extension," she asked angrily.

"No."

"Then how do you know they are getting a divorce?"

"I just know," I tried explaining. Well, that answer was not acceptable, even though it was the truth. I did just know.

This conversation taught me that it was not okay to know something without any apparent means of knowing how I knew what I knew.

In the 1970s, I was part of the new age wave that explored spirituality, personal transformation, and healing. It was the dawning of a new age. No longer living at home, I allowed my intuition to resurface.

I had my first professional psychic reading in 1979 and still have the notes she wrote for me during the session. Under the section entitled "Cosmic Purpose," she wrote: "To counsel and teach through your psychic gifts and awareness."

In the 1980s, I manufactured greeting cards and stationery. I had 125 road reps all over the United States. When I traveled to work the trade shows in my representatives' booths, I spent more time with my reps "counseling" than actually selling my product.

I didn't wear flowy dresses or dangling earrings. I wore business attire and dresses. (Pants were not acceptable attire for women in business in the early 1980s.) I was a business owner and had to look the part.

At first, I was reluctant to use my intuition and do readings. I also didn't like tapping into other people's energy, particularly those who were in emotional or physical pain. If someone was in physical pain, my body would hurt where they hurt.

One night in New York, walking back to the hotel from the convention center after the trade show had concluded for the day, I had a conversation with my guides, telling them I did not want to do this. I did not want to counsel people using my psychic abilities. Guidance had a suggestion. They would talk to the individual's guides and then talk to me, so I did not have to venture into someone's energy.

With my guides' help, I was able to comfortably counsel and do readings for those who asked for my help. Because it wasn't my energy that was being expended, I ended up energized and invigorated from the readings.

A day could consist of talking to fifty to sixty people who were in search of answers. From early in the morning to late at night, using my intuition, I did "readings." Those seven years of traveling to trade shows for eight months out of the year felt like a training of sorts. I had to learn to access information quickly while having a conversation with both my guide and the person whom I was counseling.

Fast forward to the early 1990s. I enjoyed helping those who wanted to grow, change, heal, and transform their lives and decided to set up a life coaching practice. After several years, I realized that exploration, discovery, knowledge, and awareness did not equate to change and transformation for my clients.

By 2000, I knew I needed a tool or technique that could eliminate someone's dysfunctional beliefs. That's when I read a book about Emotional Freedom Technique, EFT. That book changed me, my clients, and the way in which I conducted my sessions.

The most important aspect of EFT is the statement we make as we tap. I have written books filled with tapping statements, making tapping easy for those who don't know what to say as they tap.

Table of Contents

1   Chapter 1 – Intro

2   Chapter 2 – Quinn's Story

11   Chapter 3 – Developing Your Intuition

12   Ways in Which We Receive and/or Perceive Information

13   Exercise One

14   Possible Languages of the Universe

16   Methods of Receiving Information

17   Exercise Two

18   Using "My energy" vs "Channeled Energy"

20   Exercise Three

21   Exercise Four

22   Exercise Five

23   Exercise Six

25   Chapter 4 – Asking Questions

33   Chapter 5 – Summary

34   Chapter 6 – Beliefs and Developing Your Intuition

36   Chapter 7 EFT Tapping – Emotional Freedom Technique

36   How to Tap Short Form of EFT

38   Chapter 8 – EFT Tapping, Beliefs, and Subconscious Mind

40   Chapter 9 – How Does EFT Tapping Works?

41   Chapter 10 – Benefits of Using EFT Tapping

42   Chapter 11 – Using a Negative EFT Tapping Statement

43   Chapter 12 – EFT Tapping Statements Are Most Effective When They Agree with Current Beliefs

44   Chapter 13 – The Very First EFT Tapping Statement to Tap

45	Chapter 14 – What We Say As We Tap Is Very Important
46	Chapter 15 – One Statement per Round of EFT vs Multiple Statements per Round
49	Chapter 16 – Walking Backwards EFT (Backing Up)
50	Chapter 17 – Intensity Level
51	Chapter 18 – Yawning While Tapping and Deep Breath After Tapping
52	Chapter 19 – Integration…What Happens After Tapping
53	Chapter 20 – EFT Tapping Doesn't Work for Me
54	Chapter 21 – What To Do if an EFT Tapping Statement Does Not Clear
55	Chapter 22 – Science and EFT Tapping Research
56	Chapter 23 – Is Lowering the Cortisol Level Enough to Permanently Change Our Lives?
57	Chapter 24 – Tapping Affirmations
58	Chapter 25 – Finishing Touches – Positive Statements
60	Chapter 26 – How to Use This Book
61	Chapter 27 – EFT Tapping Statements and Journaling Pages
91	Appendix
92	General Symbolism
94	Landscape Symbols
96	Structure Symbolism
98	Basic Shapes Symbolism
101	Color Significance
103	Number Keywords
105	Charkas
124	Needs
127	Pay-offs
133	Map of Consciousness
134	Mind Chatter
137	Books by Tessa Cason

Chapter 1
Intro

Intuition is a skill that is available for anyone to learn.

Intuition is an inner knowingness, a sense without any apparent explanation or conscious reasoning. It is about perceiving and receiving information that some call a sixth sense, a hunch, or a gut feeling. Intuition is knowing without knowing.

Albert Einstein said all great achievements in science start with intuitive knowledge from which deductions are then made. Jules Henri Poincaré said it is by intuition that we discover and by logic and science that we prove. G. K. Chesterton said a person uses their intelligence to find reasons to support their intuition.

Intuition precedes logic, science, reason, and the intellect.

Within each of us is a deep wisdom, an inner knowing that can be accessed at any time. It is not authoritative, critical, judgmental, or rebellious. It does not belittle, make us feel guilty, or push us to do something we are not ready to do.

Intuition is a knowingness without any apparent way of knowing.

Our intuition can be a valuable tool when we understand the language of our intuition. Intuition has two parts to it: receiving and perceiving the information and then interpreting the information. The interpretation is the challenging aspect of being intuitive.

In sports, we teach the basics before more intricate, complicated skills. Learning the language of our intuition is the basics. When learning a new skill, practice is required to become proficient. The more we practice being intuitive, receiving and interpreting information, the more proficient we will become at being intuitive.

The more we practice, the better we become. The more languages we understand, the more accurate our interpretations can be.

The following chapters suggest ways in which we are intuitive, how to develop our intuition, and the languages of the intuition.

©Tessa Cason, 2022.

Chapter 2
Quinn's Story

My tea cools as my friend walks into Starbucks. Quinn hugs me before heading to the counter to order her own cup of tea. As she sits down, I tell her that I want to talk to her about her intuition. Previously, I had sent her an email and told her that I valued her insights. I thought she knew that a business I had intended to set up with a friend was not a good idea. However, she did not verbalize the feelings that she had. She emailed back that she thought this conversation was best to do in person.

"I know you said in the email that you thought I had some insights into starting a business with Thad. I'm not sure if I did," Quinn says.

"The last time we had tea, I shared with you a dream I had that morning that seemed so real," I start. "When you interpreted the dream, even though Thad was nowhere in the dream, nor had I mentioned Thad when telling you about the dream, you thought the dream was a 'warning' in regard to setting up a business with him."

Thinking back, Quinn finally responds, "I don't remember the dream, but I do remember the conversation that we had about the dream."

"My Guidance, my intuition, thinks you knew then that setting up a business with Thad was not such a good idea for me. It would have been great for him, but not so advantageous for me. But, you didn't say anything." Making eye contact, I add, "I want you to know that you can always share your intuitive insights with me."

Quinn had attended classes that I taught on developing your intuition. I knew that she was a newbie when it came to trusting her intuition, so I wanted her to know it was okay. I would not judge her or find fault with her insights.

She sits silently for a few minutes before responding, "I'm not sure if I did. I think that I block insights. As you know, one of my big issues is conflict, wanting to avoid conflict."

"Hmm," I mumble. "So, sharing your insights, you think it might create conflict between us?"

"Not just with you but with anyone," Quinn quickly answers.

"I know one of your top needs is belonging. [Needs are listed in the Appendix.] So, are you saying that you think having intuitive insights might separate you from someone else?"

"Not just having the insights but sharing them. If I get an insight, I feel like I am supposed to share the insight," a frustrated Quinn says.

"Okay, well, can I just say that's not necessarily true? Having insights about someone else…it's up to us to use our discernment as to what and how much we share with someone."

"I think that I block my intuition and my insights, so I am not faced with having to share the insight with the other person."

"That's very possible." I pause, then add, "I used to have a photo of my spiritual teacher in my office. When people came into my office and asked about the photo, I told them it was my spiritual teacher. I received one of three different responses. The first response was that the person who asked about the photo would start talking about the weather or anything BUT spirituality. The second response would be from someone curious about spirituality. The third response was from someone on a spiritual path and a discussion of spirituality usually followed."

"So," Quinn says before sipping her tea, "based on where someone is gives me a clue as to how and what to share in regard to my intuitive insights."

With a wide smile, I answer, "Exactly! Just because we have an insight about someone does not mean that we must share the insight. We have to use our discernment as to what we can share, how much to share, how to share the insight, and when would be the best time to share some or all of the insight."

"But, if I don't have the insights, I don't have to put myself in conflict with someone else or myself."

Shifting in my chair to face Quinn, I ask her, "How does having an insight put you in conflict with yourself, Quinn? I don't understand."

Looking down at the tea in her hands before answering, Quinn finally says, "I'm in conflict with myself about whether to share or not to share."

"Well, that leaves you in a lose-lose situation." A broad grin spreads across my face. "I can see why you don't even want to tune into your intuition."

Frowning at me, Quinn says, "But, knowing that I am blocking my intuition also puts me in conflict."

The spiritual teacher that I am was enjoying this conversation. "Well, this is a bummer. Damned if you do and damned if you don't. But, since you are blocking your intuition, I am assuming it is easier to be in conflict with yourself than with someone else," I add.

©Tessa Cason, 2022.

"True. I know you are enjoying my discomfort, aren't you," a smiling Quinn says. "Okay. I get it. With my belonging need, having an insight about someone and not knowing what to do with the insight might make me different and not fit in. So, yes, it is easier to be in conflict with myself than with someone else."

Laughing, I comment, "I know that I shouldn't, but yes, I am enjoying watching your discomfort! Sounds like you have yourself in a quandary, Quinn!"

"I agree, and it's no fun! I know that you think this is funny. It makes sense, as to the reason why I have kept my intuition at arm's length. I know that I am intuitive. I want to be intuitive. I want to develop my intuition. But, I can see that being intuitive might challenge my belonging need; thus, I play it safe by NOT being intuitive." With this proclamation, Quinn decides to get some water.

After returning to her chair, I decide to switch gears a tad. "What are your top pay-offs? [Pay-offs are listed in the Appendix.]

"Avoidance and guarantee," Quinn utters.

"Yup," I mumble.

"I know what you are going to say!"

With a twinkle in my eye, I excitedly say, "You must be a mind reader!"

"Ha. Ha. You aren't funny," a laughing Quinn announces.

Yes, the teacher in me is enjoying this conversation. "What was I going to say?"

Feeling confident in herself, Quinn explains, "With pay-offs, like avoidance and guarantee, I avoid being intuitive and sharing any intuitive hits that I have about someone until I have a guarantee that my belonging need will not be challenged."

Quinn opens her journal that she carries with her always and makes some notes.

I acknowledge my student for her correct insight and then ask, "Want to add one more factor into your being intuitive and allowing yourself to be intuitive? You know how I love triangles when it comes to cause and the result. In your journal, draw a triangle. At one point, write: 'Belonging Need.' At another point, write: 'Pay-offs of avoidance and guarantee'."

After writing what she is told to write, she looks up at me expectedly.

©Tessa Cason, 2022.

I ask, "You are an Enneagram 9, correct?"

"Correct."

Knowing that Quinn had taken a class on the Enneagrams, I ask her to give me five adjectives to describe the 9 personality.

"If I remember correctly, 9s are the peacemakers and do not like conflict. They will go along to get along."

Laughing, I say, "Well, that goes along with wanting to avoid conflict. Got it."

"9s prefer to avoid conflict." Pausing to think, Quinn then adds, "Okay, 9's basic fear is loss and separation."

"Got it. Your need for belonging. Not wanting to experience loss or separation."

"I know that peace is the opposite of conflict, but 9's desire is to be at peace with themselves, as well as with the world around them. To keep the peace, they are accepting and agreeable."

I remain quiet, allowing Quinn to reflect on her class and what she could remember.

"Oh, they are supporting and reassuring to those around them. Typically, they have problems with inertia."

I add, "Problems with inertia? That sounds like avoidance. What else about an Enneagram 9 personality? So far, we have avoids conflict, avoids loss and separation, desires peace, and can get stuck in inertia."

Defensively, Quinn says, "Don't forget loves peace, is the peacemaker, and is very supportive."

"Okay. Loves peace, is the peacemaker, and is very supportive. Anything else you want to add?"

"Yes. 9s are reliable, sturdy, and likable individuals…"

I add, "…that like to avoid conflict and loss, going along to get along."

Putting down her cup, she sits up straight and says, "Okay, I have this triangle. Now what? How do I start to develop and use my intuition?"

"Tapping. We are going to do some tapping," I explain.

I take her journal and pen and write out several tapping statements:

* I am afraid to develop my intuition.
* Being intuitive might create conflict for me.
* I don't trust my intuition.
* My need for belonging is stronger than my desire to be intuitive.
* I avoid being intuitive to avoid loss and separation.
* I am supposed to share all my intuitive hits with others.
* Being intuitive makes me different than others.
* I don't use my discernment to know who I can share my insights with.

"Tap these statements and let's meet back here in a couple of weeks to see what comes from the tapping."

The next time that I meet with Quinn, she comes in looking ragged. After ordering tea, we sit at a table in the warm sunshine. Quinn starts the conversation, saying, "Wow. It was easier to blame not using my intuition on avoiding conflict!"

Not wanting to rejoice in her discomfort, I try looking sympathetic.

"You know your sympathetic face isn't coming across as sincere, right?" Quinn says with a frown.

I shrug my shoulders, "I tried looking sympathetic. What gave me away?"

"The smile on your face. No, the smirk on your face!" she says with emphasis.

With true sincerity, I say, "Okay. Okay. Tell me what has been happening the last couple of weeks."

"Where to begin?" a confused Quinn mumbles.

I take a sip of my tea and wait for Quinn to continue. My smirk is gone, and I am truly concerned with Quinn's discomfort. I didn't want to make it worse, so I stay quiet, sending her the energy of love.

With a heavy sigh, Quinn starts, "I did the tapping. Then the mind chatter started. 'I'm not really intuitive.' 'Intuitive is nothing more than guessing.' If intuition is nothing more than my imagination, guessing, or what I want to happen, then it would be a mistake to follow the intuitive insights and hits that I get." [See Mind Chatter chapter in the Appendix.]

"And, did you do more tapping?" I inquire.

Putting down her hot tea, she says, "Yes. You have taught us how to make our mind chatter statements into tapping statements. [See in the Appendix on how to turn mind chatter into tapping statements.] So, yes, I tapped that intuition is nothing more than make-believe, guessing, and my imagination."

Leaning back, I am pleased that she turned her mind chatter into tapping statements. I wait for Quinn to continue. Her tea is still too hot to drink, so she takes a sip of water.

After the pause, Quinn adds, "I realized that I ignored my hunches, allowed fear to stop me from developing my intuition, from even sensing my intuition. And didn't think I was intuitive at all."

"Did you make these into tapping statements, as well?"

"Yes." After taking a sip of her tea, she continues. "Then, I realized that I was too logical of a person to be intuitive. Intuition doesn't make sense. Intuition isn't real. I was too much of a skeptic to believe that intuition was real. My rational mind led me back to believing that any intuitive insights were my desire of what I wanted to happen and not real. My logic mind challenged my intuitive 'hits.' I realized that I was too rational of a person to believe in intuition."

Seeing Quinn's anxiousness and nervousness, I ask if she wants to walk and talk. I thought this might help her settle down. She stands, slings her bag over her shoulder, picks up her tea, and says, "Let's walk."

I stand, sling my bag over my own shoulder, pick up my tea, and follow her out into the sunshine, toward the park. Again, I wait until she is ready to continue. I really do have compassion for her distress.

"Yes, I made those into tapping statements, as well. Being intuitive is hard. It's complicated. I might interpret the insights incorrectly. I'm not wise enough to be intuitive. Sometimes, my gut feeling doesn't make any sense. It's hard, trying to figure out what I am feeling and if what I'm feeling is my intuition or something that I'm thinking. If I can't distinguish between my thoughts and intuitive insights, how can I interpret the insights or even trust my interpretation?"

Quinn takes a long breath and remains silent for the next ten steps. I decide to jump in and make a few comments and observations. "It is true. It is difficult sometimes to know if something is your thoughts or an intuitive insight. With practice, you learn to distinguish between the two. With practice, you can learn how to interpret your insights accurately. Intuition is a skill. It's not something we are taught in school nor is it something someone is born with. There is a tendency of some to complicate the insights. Sometimes intuition is quite simple, but if the interpretation is more complicated, maybe it might have more value."

Stopping, Quinn turns toward me. "Tessa, you are the only one I know who is intuitive. No one I know is intuitive, or at least, they don't talk to me about being intuitive. I don't want to be the one to start a conversation about being intuitive. My belonging need wants to fit in and not stand out or be different than them. What if I shared with others that I thought I was intuitive and they either laugh at me or start avoiding me? I'm not sure that I want others to know I am developing my intuition."

I face Quinn and say, "It's possible that others could be threatened. Others may misunderstand what intuition is about. I've had people tell me being intuitive is evil, that intuition comes from the devil."

I take her arm, turn her back toward the path, and begin walking again. "Quinn, you can ignore your intuition. It's your choice."

Taking a deep breath, Quinn begins, "I'm afraid that if I am intuitive, it will lead to heartache. I don't want to know if someone is dying. I know this fear clouds my insights and interpretations. Sometimes, I soak up people's energy. This isn't something I want to get lost in."

I wonder if this is the time to dive into such a topic. Thinking, I take a sip of my tea and decide to address this concern, since it is on her mind. "It is possible that we could know about someone's health. Not often, but it is possible. Let's say you did sense that someone's health was at risk. What would you do?"

After a nervous laugh, Quinn says, "Freak out."

"And then what," I ask.

"After I freaked out, what would I do?"

"Yup, after you freaked out."

Quinn sees a park bench up ahead and decides now would be a good time to sit down. Her restlessness and anxiety seem to have simmered into confusion and tiredness. "Truthfully, I don't know, Tessa. How would I know if what I was sensing was the truth?"

Sitting beside Quinn, both of us looking out over the expansive park, feeling the warmth from the sun, slowly, I say, "Remember my example last time about determining where someone was to know how to gauge a conversation—the photo of my spiritual teacher?"

Softly, Quinn says, "I do."

"Sometimes I call it 'fishing.' If I sensed that someone might have a health challenge, I might ask how their health is. If they change the topic, I know the topic is not one that they would be comfortable talking about; thus, I follow their lead. Sometimes, people just need to be heard. They don't always want answers or solutions. They want someone to hear their concerns. I can show them compassion and empathy and hear their concerns without needing to offer a solution."

"Does it happen often?" whispers Quinn.

"No. It hasn't," I answer truthfully.

Quinn sits very still, deep in thought. I finish my tea, stand up, walk to a trash receptacle, and drop in my cup. When I return, Quinn comments, "Tessa, I don't trust the accuracy of my insights. I wouldn't want to cause someone else heartache."

"I sense that you feel your insights are supposed to be huge revelations for someone."

Quinn pauses before she confesses that she thinks this could be true. "I am beginning to realize that my willingness to develop my intuition, to honor my intuition, is complicated by what I think is expected of me and the messages that my intuition has for me, as well as for other people."

"That's insightful," I tease, as I stretch out my legs in front of me.

Playfully, Quinn says, "Do intuitive insights come with instructions of what to do with them?"

"Adding levity to our conversation? Getting too heavy for you?" I joke.

With a huge grin, leaning back on the bench, she says, "Did it work?"

We both watch as a young man, obviously a dog walker, struggles with ten leashes, ten excited dogs pulling to pick up their messages on every stone, tree, blade of grass, and shrub within their reach.

Once he has moved beyond our view, Quinn says, "I get it, Tessa. There are many different issues that someone could have with being intuitive, developing their intuition, and feeling responsible for the insights that they receive. Until a lot of these issues are cleared, our perception might not be accurate. I did a lot of tapping these last two weeks. I am ready now to develop this skill and practice."

We stand and head back to the coffee shop. "Quinn, there is one thing that I do want to add in regard to someone else. We don't always know what someone else's lessons are. We don't want someone else telling us how to live our life. It's not our place to tell someone else how to live theirs.

©Tessa Cason, 2022.

"In regard to ourselves, our intuition can be a valuable tool. There is a place for the logical mind, as well as the intuitive mind, in our lives. Sometimes, our intuition is the quiet voice within. Sometimes, it is a feeling. Sometimes, we might think of someone, and then the phone rings and it is them on the other end.

"When Mike died, I found dimes every day for a week. Now, when I know that Mike is around me, I find dimes.

"I know when something is a Truth because I either yawn, tear up, or get goosebumps. I know that it is my intuition telling me to pay attention. For me, I know my intuition is helping me to live a more fulfilled and content life. Growth is one of my top needs. I know my intuition is helping me discover my ah-ha wisdom to heal, grow, and evolve."

Walking by my side, Quinn asks, "Then you trust your intuition. How long did that take?"

Looping my arm through hers, I respond, "A long time. The information that we receive is correct. It's our interpretation of the insights or feelings that takes time and lots of practice. We need to learn the language of our intuition. I learned about numerology, the significance of colors, astrology, symbolism, spiritual cards, and other modalities. It was easier to interpret the information once I started to study their language. I have several handouts that I shared in class. I will send you digital copies of some of the handouts." [In the Appendix.]

With a lighter heart and step, Quinn looks around and marvels at how clear and sharp everything looks. For the first time in two weeks, she finally feels at peace and is ready to start a new chapter in her life, her growth, and her evolution.

Chapter 3
Developing Your Intuition

What is intuition?
Is there a difference between being intuitive and being psychic?

* Intuition is an inner knowingness, a sense, without any apparent explanation or conscious reasoning, a gut feeling.

* Psychic is defined as perceiving, receiving, or transferring information without the use of the five common senses... sight, touch, hearing, taste, smell.

Are they the same? I think so. For the purpose of this book, I will use "intuitive" and "intuition."

Everyone is intuitive.
Intuition is a skill, just like riding a bike.

The more we practice riding a bike, the better we become. Riding in different terrains, different climates, and diverse weather conditions prepare us for the different terrains, climates, and weather conditions we could find ourselves cycling. The more we practice, the better we become. The more we are prepared for, the better we will do.

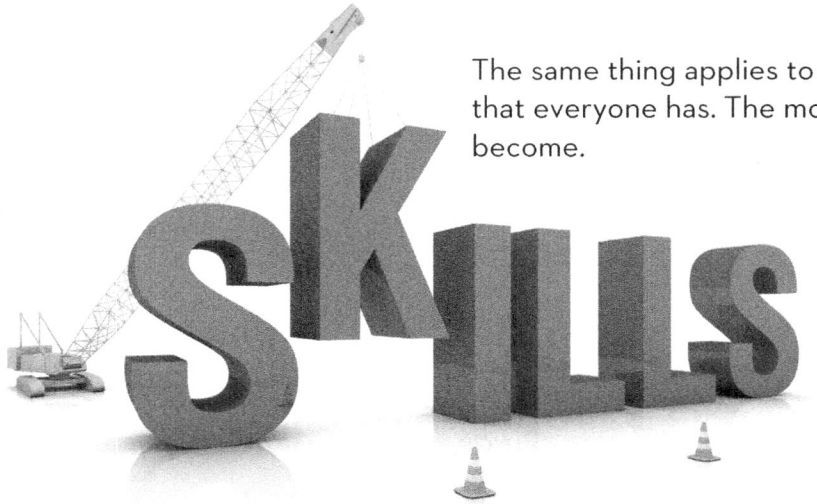

The same thing applies to our intuition. Intuition is a skill that everyone has. The more we practice, the better we become.

©Tessa Cason, 2022.

Ways in which we receive and/or perceive information

Visual, also called Clairvoyance, clear seeing:

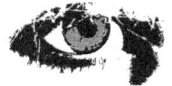  Some will see the information in their mind's eye. It might be a color, an animal, a person, a car, a symbol, an event, a tree, a calendar, a book. A clairvoyant sees in pictures.

Auditory, also called Clairaudience, clear hearing:

Some will gather information through what they hear. It could be a song, a melody, a person's voice, everyday sounds such as a car driving away, a dog barking, birds chirping, children playing, a school bell.

We could receive information from unseen friends, counselor, guides, angels. How do we know the difference between our voice and their voice? Sometimes, the two voice may not sound different. Sometimes it may sound very different: different dialect, different tempo, different words than ones we normally use. If the "voice" sounds like our own, discernment is required.

Kinesthetic, also called Clairsentience, clear sensing:

 Some will have a feeling, a sense, a knowingness, an inner hunch...we know without any visible means of knowing what we know.

Chills, goose bumps, yawns, and/or tearing up can be confirmation of what we are hearing, thinking, seeing is a Truth.

Each of us has one dominant method of receiving information, visual, auditory, and/or kinesthetic.
Once we develop that which is the most dominant for us, the other two will follow and be developed as well.

©Tessa Cason, 2022.

Exercise One

* Close your eyes. Take a few deep breaths and relax.

* Imagine yourself walking along the shore of a beautiful, pristine lake. You have the lake to yourself and enjoy the silence.

* It's a warm comfortable summer day. You lift your face up to feel the warm rays of the sun.

* From a distance, you can hear the quacking of ducks. As the sounds get louder, you look over to see the ducks splash land on the water. You watch as the ducks ruffle their feathers, dip their heads into the water, and flap their wings and shake.

* You continue to stroll down the shore, moving in and out of the water. The water feels cool on your warm feet.

* In the silence you hear all the whispers of the area…the waves gently rolling onto the beach, the breeze rustling through the trees, and your own breath as you inhale and exhale.

What was the most predominate method in which you experienced the visualization above? Did you see the lake, the ducks, the waves, the trees? Did you hear the quacking of the ducks splash land, the breeze rustling through the trees, the waves rolling onto the beach? Did you feel the warmth of the sun rays, the cool water against your warm feet?

What was the primary method? Visual? Auditory? Kinesthetic?

©Tessa Cason, 2022.

Possible Languages of Our Intuition

Our intuition has its own language that we might want to learn. Everything has significance...

Colors: Yellow is the intellect as well as sunshine and happiness. Green is growth and the heart chakra. (Have you ever wondered why legal pads are yellow?)

Numbers: 5 is about change and unpredictability, 9 is about completions.

5

Good luck symbols: Four leaf clovers, horseshoes.

Animals and birds: The hummingbird is a symbol of joy, the butterfly is for transformation, the dog is faithful and loyal.

Astrological planets: Mercury is about communication and transportation. Saturn is the teacher.

Astrological signs: Gemini is an air sign, the intellect of the zodiac. Taurus is the bull, very stubborn when they want to be.

Astrological elements: Water symbolizes emotions. Fire symbolizes spontaneity. Fire and water together create steam when in balance. Steam engines are powerful. Too much water puts the fire out. Too little water and the fire burns uncontrollably.

Celtic symbols, Chinese symbols, Native American symbols, Egyptian symbols: Each culture has significant symbols. The Celtic cross is a bridge between the earthly and spiritual worlds. The Ankh is an Egyptian cross symbolizing a mythical eternal life, rebirth, and the life-giving power of the sun.

Cards of the Tarot: The Tower Card symbolizes abrupt and sudden changes.

Cheryl Richardson's Self-care Cards: Fifty-two inspirational self-care cards, cards such as "Dreams...Think Big! There are unseen forces ready to support your dreams." "Clearing...Clear the Clutter. When in doubt, throw it out."

©Tessa Cason, 2022.

Doreen Virtue's Healing with the Angels Oracle Cards: Forty-four card deck that includes cards such as Spiritual Growth, Emerging, Divine Timing, Trust, and Power.

Body parts: The blood represents joy. It is representative of our "tribe," our family system. In the womb, we are connected to our mother through the blood system and the family DNA and history. Difficulties of the blood might have to do with giving, receiving, and sharing of love, and/or emotional involvement and the expression of love.

Love symbols: The apple is a symbol of ecstasy, fertility, and abundance as well as love. The triangle in Ancient Egypt was seen as a symbol of intelligence and indicated the capacity for love.

Chakras: 1st chakra, the root chakra, has to do with our survival and basic needs.

Gemstones: Rutilated quartz illuminates the soul, cleanses and energizes, removes barriers to spiritual growth, and filters negative energy. Sapphire contributes to mental clarity and perception as well as promotes financial rewards.

Shapes: Circles symbolize wholeness, completeness, and calmness. A square symbolizes balance and stability.

Trees: The cherry tree symbolizes the phoenix, rising from the ashes. The willow tree is a magical and healing tree.

Archangels: Michael is in charge of protection, courage, strength, truth, and integrity. Raphael is a powerful healer and assists with all forms of healing, both humans and animals.

Angels: Elijah is the Angel of Innocence. Nathaniel is the Angel of Fire.

Pay-off for not creating our reality: Guarantee, self-pity, avoidance, blame, self-righteous, self-importance, and clinging to the past.

There are other languages besides those listed above. Consider developing a notebook of those that have significance to you.

©Tessa Cason, 2022.

Methods of Receiving Information

A. Going within/Perceiving using Visual, Auditory, or Kinesthetic

Each of us has one dominant method of receiving information, visual, auditory, and/or kinesthetic. Once we develop that which is the most dominant for us, the other two will eventually be developed as well.

B. Psychometry

Psychometry is a method in which something personal and of value of the other person is held. It could be a piece of jewelry, keys, a piece of clothing, and/or a wallet.

C. Holding hands

Some people are able to access information by holding hands.

D. Crystals and Gemstones

Some people like using crystals and/or gemstones. The quartz crystal amplifies energy. Crystals can assist with peace, creativity, intuition, perceptiveness, and understanding. Either person can hold the crystals and/or gemstones.

E. Birth date

For some people, they find it easier to tune into someone's energy by knowing the birth date of the person they are "reading." If you know astrology, it might make it easier to "pick out" the individual's energy.

F. Picture

Some people find it easier to look at a picture of the individual they are "reading."

Helpful Hint: Present Time.

It is important that we be in present time. Anger is the past. Fear is the future. If we are not in present time, we are either in the anger of the past or fear of the future. The information we are perceiving and receiving when we are not in present time is through dirty "filters" and thus, would lack accuracy.

©Tessa Cason, 2022.

Helpful Hint: Two Aspects to Intuition.

First is receiving information (always accurate) and secondly, interpreting the information (not always so accurate). Learning to interpret the information takes loads of practice!

Exercise Two

The intent of this exercise is to:

1. Determine which of the methods described is most comfortable for you.

2. To work through the retrieved information with your partner to better understand and interpret the information.

Need a partner. Designate an A and a B. Each person should collect an object of significance from the other person (B from previous page) as well as a picture (F). If no picture is available, pull out your driver's license (for those that have one). If any crystals or gemstones are available (D), select some to use for this experiment. Find out each other's birth date (E).

A is the "reader" and B is the one being "read." "A" needs to be in present time. Do not judge the information as to correctness and validity.

Person A asks person B for permission to "read" their energy. Without permission, we are intruding and the information could be compromised.

Person A has this question in mind: "Show me a season, summer, winter, fall, or spring, significant to this person and why." Try each of the methods above without speaking any of the information out loud, yet.

A. What information can you see, hear, or sense?

B. Take the object that person B supplied that was significant to them.

C. Hold hands with person B.

D. Pick up the crystal or gemstone selected.

E. Focus on person B's birth date.

F. Focus your attention on their picture.

©Tessa Cason, 2022.

After you have completed all of the above, determine which one felt most comfortable; which one you received more information.

Once you have gone through all the methods and have received, retrieved, and accessed information, share with your partner what you discovered. If you don't understand something you received, ask the other person if it has any significance and meaning for them. They will help you understand what you received.

Once you have shared all the information, switch.

The information each received, perceived, and shared was correct. *We may not understand or be able to interpret the information as of yet.* The more we understand the language of our intuition, the more significance the information will have.

Helpful Hint: Higher Altitudes

David Hawkins has a Map of Consciousness, ranging from Shame at 20, to Enlightenment at 1000. In the lower altitudes, we are in levels of Shame, Anger, and Guilt. 250 is Neutrality, the beginning of the higher altitudes. As we move into the higher altitudes, the "filters" we view the world through are **less cluttered**. Being in Neutrality or higher will improve our intuitive interpretations and impressions. (See Appendix for more info on David Hawkins' Map of Consciousness.)

How does one move up to the higher altitudes? By doing emotional growth work and by "deleting" dysfunctional beliefs on the subconscious level. EFT, Emotional Freedom Technique, is very effective at deleting the beliefs that keep us tied to the lower altitudes.

Using My Energy vs Channeled Energy

My preference is to use channeled energy from a higher consciousness source. This means nothing more than asking for assistance from a higher consciousness source and allowing the information to come through me, much like a television channel broadcasts a program through the air waves.

When we use our energy to gather information, I have found that many "readers" feel drained and thus, reach for food to fill the exhaustion. The food does not eliminate the exhaustion. It just adds pounds to the body. Meditation, quiet time, and exercise can restore that which was drained.

How does one ask for assistance and guidance? With sincerity, appreciation, love, gratitude, acceptance, and an open heart while still being discerning, astute, and perceptive.

From "whom" do I ask for assistance? The who is up to us. We could ask our guides, Archangel Michael, a wise sage, and/or an angel. Establish a rapport with whoever has been chosen to be a counselor.

Dialoguing with our counselors can be done verbally, writing in a journal, while on a walk, in meditation, silently while sitting at our desk...anywhere, anytime.

When we begin to work with a guide, a counselor, it is not about "trusting" them completely. It is about establishing a relationship with our counselor, one in which both of us are equals and equal contributors. Carry on a dialogue with them. Talk to them as you would talk to others. They have to "prove" themselves to us.

When I was a swim coach, the mother of one of my swimmer's came to me and asked if I would talk to her son, Eric. It seemed as if Eric did not see any reason to learn certain things, like spelling and math. I found this nine year old's reasoning fascinating. "I will have a secretary or a computer that will spell for me. Math, I will have a calculator in my wristwatch." This was way before computers were the necessities they are today.

I asked Eric if he didn't know math, how he could be sure the answer on his calculator was correct and he didn't make a mistake entering the numbers. If he was reading a report and didn't know how to spell, would he know the difference between deer and dear, steel and steal? One wrong punch on his calculator could result in a disaster. One letter could change the whole meaning of a word. Was he willing to blindly trust his secretary and/or anyone he might be negotiating with?

The idea of blind trust did not appeal to Eric. He wanted to be in control of his life. He realized the best way to be prepared was to learn math and spelling. Mom was thrilled.

The idea of blind trust should not appeal to anyone in this regard or any other. An unseen friend, counselors, guides, just because they exist on another level does not ensure Truth and validity. The world, both seen and unseen, is full of tricksters and the unreliable sort. Trust is about trusting our ability to discern.

As in the beginning of any relationship, certain procedures, styles, protocols, routines, idiosyncrasies have to be worked out. Learn about the unseen guides/counselors.

©Tessa Cason, 2022.

Establish a dialogue and you determine if this is someone you would choose to work with and if they can be trusted. How does it feel? Does it feel calming? Comfortable? If you feel uncomfortable, not quite centered, you might want to try working with someone else.

Helpful Hint: Be the Observer of the participant.

We are both the participant and the observer. If we are attached to the information we perceive, it is difficult to know if the information is what we want it to be, or a true knowing.

Learn not to take and make things personal.

When you are around other people, can you sense their energy? Can you sense your own? Are they giving you energy? Are they sucking your energy?

Exercise Three

Try the exercise again after you have established a rapport
and a relationship with your guide/counselor/angel:

Designate an A and a B partner. Collect an object of significance from each person as well as a picture, crystals or gemstones, and find out each other's birth date. A is the "reader" and B is the one being "read." Be in present time. Do not judge the information. Ask for permission.

Person A asks for their counselor to be present and for their assistance. Person A has the same question in mind, "Show me a season, summer, winter, fall or spring, significant to this person and why." Go through each of the six methods as before. Do not share any of the information until you have gone through all the methods.

A. What information can you see, hear, or sense?

B. Take the object that person B supplied that was significant to them.

C. Hold hands with person B.

D. Pick up the crystal or gemstone selected.

E. Focus on person B's birth date.

F. Focus your attention on their picture.

©Tessa Cason, 2022.

Once again, after going through all of the methods and have received, retrieved, and accessed information, share with your partner what you discovered.

After you have completed all of the above, determine the difference for you between working with a guide and not working with a guide.

Switch and allow B to be the reader.

Helpful Hint: Personalize Your Higher Self

* Our Higher Self has their own name and persona.
* See how they are dressed.
* Discover as much as you can about your Higher Self.

Exercise Four

Write Out a Question on a Note Card

* Take a few deep breaths.
* Write out your question on a note card.
* Hold the note card in your hand or hands.
* Notice if you have any sensations in your body? Where and what type of sensation? Knot in your stomach? Tension in your chest? Feel nervous or restless? A peaceful feeling spreading over your whole body?
* Do any words pop into your mind? Excitement? Doubt? Insecurity? Triumphant?
* Any images flash through your mind? A gate? A mountain top? Babbling brook?
* What color comes to mind? Sky blue? Fire engine red? Hot pink?
* What animal comes to mind? Seahorse? Dragon? Unicorn?
* What physical location in the world comes to mind? Floating down the Nile? Climbing Machu Picchu? Relaxing on Maui? On a safari in Africa?
* Write your discoveries on the note card.
* Write out the significance of each of your discoveries.

    A knot in my stomach could indicate nervousness.

    Excitement. The outcome would excite me.

    The gate could signify I am beginning a new phase.

    Fire engine red...excitement again.

    Unicorn...magical.

©Tessa Cason, 2022.

Interpret the Discoveries

* Begin speaking immediately. If you delay, the logical mind with take over.
* Make a story out of what you discovered.

I am nervousness about starting something new in my life. At my age, I might be past my prime. Though, this new path and new phase of my life is exciting, it might be too much for me. On the other hand, it could be magical.

Helpful Hint: Weave the information into a story.

When interpreting information and/or insights, weave the information/insights into a story. Begin speaking immediately. If you delay, the logical mind will take over. Hear, sense, or see the information as you speak. Most likely, more information will be heard or seen or felt as you do.

Exercise Five

Need Cheryl Richardson's *Self-Care Cards* or Doreen Virtue's *Healing with the Angels Card* deck.

Method one:
* Think of your question or something that you want clarification on. You can also write out the question.
* Pull five cards. Keep the cards face down and stack one on top of the other.
* Turn over the bottom (first drawn) card. This is the "theme" of the reading.
* Cards two, three, and four (drawn) relate to the theme. As you turn over each card, start telling a story.
* If you are able to fulfill/complete cards two, three, and four, the fifth card is the possible outcome.

Method Two:

Lay out all five cards and make a story out of the five cards, regardless of the order in which the cards were drawn.

© Tessa Cason, 2022.

Helpful Hint: Carry a Journal with you to write down your insights and "hits."

Get an insight, write it down. You may not understand how to interpret the information at this time, but write it down.

Journal your random thoughts, your insights, your ah-ha moments, your interpretations.

Devote time each day to "listening" to, observing, and journaling your thoughts.

Write down any and all ideas that come to mind during the day.

Exercise Six

Have a Conversation (verbal or written) with Your Higher Self and/or Guidance

Verbal:
* When you need advice, clearly and in detail, outline your problem in your mind's eye.
* Take a few deep breaths, relax, ask for guidance, and see or sense your consciousness aligning with the center of your being, with your inner wisdom.
* When you return to a wide awake and alert state, pay attention to the first thought(s) you have.

Written:
* Have a problem? Need advice? Have a written conversation with your Guide, Archangel, an Angel, and/or your Higher Self about the problem.
* Ask if they can help or counsel you.
* Close your eyes, take a few deep breaths, and relax.
* Once you are relaxed and centered, open your eyes, and begin writing.
* Write whatever comes to mind without judgment.

Helpful Hint: Practice daily. Keep learning the language of your intuition.

When learning the language of your intuition, consider making note cards to assist in your learning. For example, when learning about numbers or colors, on one note card, write out the attributes for an individual number or color.

© Tessa Cason, 2022.

Helpful Hint: Where Does Intuition Come From

IT can come from our higher self, angels, guides, as well as tricksters (someone that may want to sabotage). It is a learning process to discern where your information and insights might be coming from.

* To begin, set the intent of whom you want to converse with...Higher Self, Archangel Gabriel, a Guide, and/or anyone else that could be helpful.

* Initiate a connection and began a dialogue with your Guidance.

© Tessa Cason, 2022.

Chapter 4
Asking Questions

1. **Be as specific and clear as possible.**

A friend asks: "Would you like to go to the movies?"

After you answer, "Yes, I would," they walk away. You're left wondering what happened.

Your friend wasn't very specific or clear. They asked about the activity of going to the movies, but they didn't include "when." The "when" could be specific, like "Saturday night," or vague, like "sometime."

The friend also didn't include with "whom" you are going to the movies. With them? A group of people? Maybe the "with me" was implied. Not being specific leaves you wondering.

The question is: "Would you like to go to the movies with me on Saturday night?" This question is clear and specific.

2. **Only ask one aspect of a question at a time.**

    Question: Go to the concert with Tina tomorrow night?
      This question has three parts to it.
       * Go to the concert
       * With Tina
       * Tomorrow night

If any part of the answer is "No," the whole answer will be "No." Or the answer might be "Yes," but confusion results when the evening did not go as planned.

3. **Be neutral.**

Really wanting an answer to be "Yes" or "No" can influence the answer.

During one of my classes, one of the students decided that he would calibrate himself on the Map of Consciousness. When he calibrated himself at "Enlightenment," the highest calibration on the map, I started laughing.

He turned toward me, smiled, and said, "Maybe I wasn't being neutral."

© Tessa Cason, 2022.

4. Use "should" questions sparingly.

In class, a student asked herself a question: Should I break up with my boyfriend? When the answer was "Yes," she looked at me with dismay. "But, I don't want to break up with my boyfriend," she said. "Why would my intuition tell me to break up with him?"

This was a great teaching example for the whole class on using "should" in the question.

I asked the student, "What do you really want to know?"

She pondered the question for a few minutes then responded, "I guess I'm wanting to know if I am going to get my heart broken. If I break up with him before that happens, my heart won't get broken."

"Do you like this guy," I asked.

"I do. Probably more than any other guy I have dated. That's why I think I should break up with him before he ends the relationship."

I was left confused by her logic. It certainly wasn't sound and seemed as if she was making plenty of assumptions.

I asked, "If you like the guy and you broke up with him, wouldn't that break your heart?"

"I guess it would. I don't want to get hurt."

"Maybe the question isn't about breaking up. You might want to explore the reasons why you think he might end the relationship or the reasons why you want to give up a relationship that is fulfilling or maybe what your fears are in a relationship that you enjoy."

Another student asked, "How could she have worded the question?"

A discussion followed with the students, each offering how she could ask what she really wanted to know.

5. Consider using a rating scale of 1-10.

Example:

You: I'm considering changing companies. I've been offered a position with another company. I would be doing the same job that I am currently doing in HR. The industry is different, more or less, but the responsibilities are the same.

© Tessa Cason, 2022.

Tessa: Would this be a lateral move?

You: Yes.

Tessa: What is your question?

You: Well, would it be beneficial to change jobs?

Tessa: Beneficial financially, work conditions, work environment, or emotionally?

You: All of the above.

Tessa: Rank each job, current and potential, on a scale of 1-10, based on each of the benefits. On a scale of 1-10, with 1 being the lowest, how fulfilling would this new job be?

Example:

You: I want to know if my health will improve by pursuing this treatment.

Tessa: What about asking on a scale of 1-10: If I pursue this treatment, how beneficial would the treatment be for my physical health?

Example:

You: I want to know if this supplement is beneficial for my health.

Tessa: You can ask on a scale of 1-10: How beneficial would a supplement be for the improvement of my health?

Besides supplements, we can rate different therapists, programs, and/or books, in regard to how beneficial they might be for our health, personal growth, or whatever the objective might be.

7. Wording of a question could determine the validity and accuracy of an answer.

Let's look more in-depth at an inquiry that you might have. Remember:

1) Wording is critical
2) Be as specific as possible
3) Singularly focused

Example:

Let's say you ask the question: Should I move cross country to live with my boyfriend?

The answer that you received was a "Yes." You moved cross country. Spent all your savings moving and now have a zero balance in your bank accounts. After a month of looking for a job, you are still unemployed, and your boyfriend ends the relationship, asking you to move out.

You have no place to live, no income to afford another place to live, and no means of returning home. Yikes! "But…when I tested, the answer was a yes!"

1) There really are no "shoulds." If you have a belief that the only way you can learn is through pain and struggle, you probably learned a lot from this experience!

2) This question has multiple parts to it.
    a) Move cross country
    b) Live with my boyfriend

When asking questions, it is best to be as singularly focused as possible.

Let's re-examine this question: Should I move cross country to live with my boyfriend?

Tessa: What is the objective, goal, or intent of your question?

You: To know if I would be happy moving cross country to live with my boyfriend.

T: Are there other factors involved in this inquiry?

Y: Well, yes. It is a necessity for me to get a job as quickly as possible. My boyfriend doesn't want to support me. He wants me to share the expenses. It will take most, if not all, of the money that I have to move. I will need to get a job as soon as possible.

T: Have you looked into how easy this might be?

Y: Yes. I've looked in the paper and online.

T: Have you spent an extended period of time with your boyfriend, in his space?

Y: Yes. For our vacations, I usually fly cross country to spend time with him. The longest I have stayed was for two weeks. Everything worked out well.

T: Define "happy".

Y: Happy. Well, I do understand that no relationship is trouble-free. All relationships will have problems. When they happen, it is important to negotiate a solution.

T: Have the two of you had to negotiate anything in the past?

Y: Yes.

T: And how did that go?

Y: It was interesting. He wanted his way, typical man, you know. He pouted, got angry, and would not talk to me until I finally gave in.

T: Does that work for you?

Y: Well, sometimes. I realize that I need to compromise. I can't always have my way.

T: Is marriage important to you?

Y: Yes.

T: And for him?

Y: It is not as important to him as it is to me. He's still thinking about whether he wants to be married.

T: This is okay with you that he doesn't know if he ever wants to marry?

Y: Yes. I think, well…I am hoping that once we live together for a while, he will not want to spend the rest of his life without me. Wishful thinking, I know. My eyes are wide open.

T: Define for me again the object of your inquiry?

Y: I can see that has changed. I would like to know if it is worth the gamble to move cross country and set up house with this man.

T: Everything is a risk and a gamble in life.

Y: Okay. Not definite enough.

T: Can you break your inquiry down into categories?

Y: Actually, I can. One has to do with finding a job and the monetary arena. The other is the relationship.

T: Which is the most important?

Y: That's a toughie. It is important to him that I pay half, pay my share. He doesn't want to support me. Moving cross country will drain all my funds. The relationship is equally as important.

T: Which is primary? Would you be looking for a job in that area if he were not living there?

Y: No. So, I need to determine if the relationship is good enough for me to leave behind everything I have here.

T: Good enough?

Y: Satisfying? Fulfilling? Worthwhile?

T: How about thinking more long-term, more workable, doable, feasible, or viable?

Y: Okay. I get ya. I'm thinking more emotionally. You are thinking more practically. My head is up in the clouds. You have your feet on the ground.

T: Which is more important to you?

Y: Actually, more practical. Feet on the ground would be best. When my head is up in the clouds, it is difficult to see reality.

T: So, what is the real need? What is your objective now?

Y: I need to know if this relationship is strong enough to endure the everyday stresses of life.

T: The relationship? You or him?

Y: There is a difference, isn't there. Okay. Each of us in this relationship, with each other.

T: Anything else? Any other objectives? Any other needs?

Y: I guess, I would like to know if we do live together, will he get bored or will he want us to be together for a lifetime? Rather than assuming that he will feel as I hope he would feel, it might be better if I knew before I moved. I have been hesitant to ask him. Now, I see it is better to deal with reality—what is real rather than make-believe or what I hope will be. It is my responsibility to take care of myself and not assume that everyone else will also have the same objective to take care of me.

© Tessa Cason, 2022.

T: Well stated. This can be your intent with this inquiry. The intent can be that you are responsible for yourself, your well-being, and your happiness. You stated earlier your need. You stated that you needed to know if this relationship is strong enough to endure the everyday stresses of life. Your objective then is to make the wisest decision at this time with the information that you can gather.

Y: Sounds good to me.

T: Let's make a list of the questions now.

Y: Okay.

1. Living together under the same roof, this relationship can comfortably handle the stresses of everyday life. (You can add: "To a level of five or higher.")

2. Living together under the same roof, I can comfortably handle the stresses of everyday life, with this man. (You can add: "To a level of five or higher.")

3. We can successfully negotiate the stresses of everyday life and conflicts with each other.

4. Our styles of handling conflict are compatible with each other.

5. Within the first six months of living together, I will be bored and/or lose interest in this relationship.

6. Within the first six months of living together, I will be bored and/or lose interest in him.

7. Our styles of handling money are compatible with each other.

There are certainly many more questions that can be asked in regard to this question.

8. There is a reason that we ask the questions we do. The reasons are our objectives.

It is important to know the objective when asking questions. Vague, unclear questions with inconclusive answers will have you thinking your intuition isn't accurate. The issue may not be your intuition. The issue may be the wording of your inquiry!

Conclusion:

Intuition is a skill that anyone can learn.

A friend in college was a mystery shopper for Jack in the Box drive-thru restaurants. He asked if I wanted to be a mystery shopper. (A mystery shopper is a consumer, just like everyone else. The store employees do not know that they are being evaluated. That's the mystery part.)

When I turned in my first shop, I said the hamburger was good. My friend called me into his office and said, "Good?"

"Yes," I answered.

"Wrong. Were the tomatoes fresh, was the lettuce crisp, was the bun warm, was there enough sauce on the bun?"

"Oh, more details."

If our questions are vague, it will be difficult to know if the answers that we receive are correct. The more details, the more specific and focused the question, the crisper the answers will be.

© Tessa Cason, 2022.

Chapter 5
Summary

Intuition is something that we can use constantly. It is always available and ongoing. It is a part of us, who we are, how we make decisions, our discernment, and our being.

* It does take practice on our part.
* It does require that we learn the language of our intuition.
* It does require that we strive to maintain the higher altitudes on David Hawkins' Map of Consciousness.
* It does require that we be the observer and detach from the information we receive.
* It does require that we suspend our judgments and not to judge the information that we see, feel, or hear.
* It requires patience with ourselves while we are learning a new skill.
* It does require us to go with the flow, to receive, and to be in present time.
* We will have one primary method of accessing information. As we develop the primary, the other two will follow as well.
* Know that what you see, feel, and/or hear is accurate. Our interpretation of that information takes time and practice.
* Weave the information into a story.
* By telling ourselves we are not intuitive, we won't be.
* We need to learn how to distinguish our "voice" from our guides voice if we work with counselors, guides, angels, and/or any other unseen guide.
* Cold chills, goose bumps, tearing up, lump in the throat, yawning can be confirmation of Truth.
* Stay inquisitive.
* If the information is about someone else, if you don't understand what you are seeing, hearing, or feeling, ask the other person if it has significance to them.
* It does require practice, practice, and more practice.
* When asking questions, ask "what" and "how" questions rather than "when," "will," and "why" questions.
* Be specific and clear when asking questions.
* Only ask one aspect of the question at one time. Be as singularly focused as possible.
* Remain neutral when asking questions.

© Tessa Cason, 2022.

Chapter 6
Beliefs and Developing Your Intuition

In most society, being intuitive is thought not to be real, have no value, and/or to be evil. Hearing and experiencing these "beliefs" throughout our lives could create blocks to being intuitive. Over the years, you might have had "intuitive insights," or "hunches" that you ignored and, now you want to develop your intuition and are not able to.

Do you let fear stop you? Fear of what you might see, hear, or know? Fear of being wrong and making a mistake if you act on your intuition and your intuition wasn't accurate? And now, you are afraid to be intuitive, your fear stops you from being intuitive?

Do you trust your intuition and it didn't turn out so well and now you don't trust your intuition at all?

Does learning the language of your intuition seem overwhelming and too hard? Can you not make sense of what your intuition is showing you and thus end up confused and thinking your intuition doesn't make sense?

Are you too logical and rational to be intuitive? Sometimes logical people are the most intuitive once they learn the language of their intuition.

Some fear that if they are intuitive, they will soak up other people's negative energy and, thus do not want to be intuitive.

Some think that you are either born with intuition or not and that it is not a skill that can be learned. That's a bummer for them.

Some think intuition doesn't work for them. The first time they picked up a baseball bat, were they able to hit the ball? Or after lots of practice, were they finally able to hit the ball?

All of the above are beliefs that could block someone from developing their intuition. Are you that someone? If you are, there is something you can do to heal the blocks to developing your intuition. It is called EFT Tapping, Emotional Freedom Technique.

The next section is information about EFT Tapping followed by 300 EFT Tapping statements that can be tapped or combined into tapping scripts.

© Tessa Cason, 2022.

EFT TAPPING

Chapter 7
EFT Tapping – Emotional Freedom Technique

EFT Tapping is a very easy technique to learn. It involves making a statement as we contact the body by either circling or tapping.

An EFT Tapping Statement has three parts:

Part 1: starts with "**Even though**" followed by

Part 2: a statement which could be the **dysfunctional emotion or belief**, and

Part 3: ends with "**I totally and completely accept myself.**"

A complete statement would be, "**Even though I fear change, I totally and completely accept myself.**"

Instruction for the Short Form of EFT Tapping

The instructions below are for using the right hand. Reverse the directions to tap using the left hand. It is more effective, when we tap, to tap only one side rather than both.

I. SET UP – BEGIN WITH CIRCLING OR TAPPING THE SIDE OF THE HAND:

A. With the fingertips of the right hand, find a tender spot below the left collar bone. Once the tender spot is identified, press firmly on the spot, moving the fingertips in a circular motion toward the left shoulder, toward the outside, clockwise. Tapping the side of the hand can also be used instead of the circling.

B. As the fingers circle and press against the tender spot or tap the side of the hand, repeat the tapping statement three times: "Even though,＿＿[tapping statement]＿＿, I totally and completely accept myself." An example would be: "Even though I fear change, I totally and completely accept myself."

Side of the hand

Tender spot below the left collar bone

© Tessa Cason, 2022.

II. Tapping:

A. After the third time, tap the following eight points, repeating the [tapping statement] at each point. Tap each point five – ten times:
1. The inner edge of the eyebrow, just above the eye. [I fear change.]
2. Temple, just to the side of the eye. [I fear change.]
3. Just below the eye (on the cheekbone). [I fear change.]
4. Under the nose. [I fear change.]
5. Under the lips. [I fear change.]
6. Under the knob of the collar bone. [I fear change.]
7. Three inches under the arm pit. [I fear change.]
8. Top back of the head. [I fear change.]

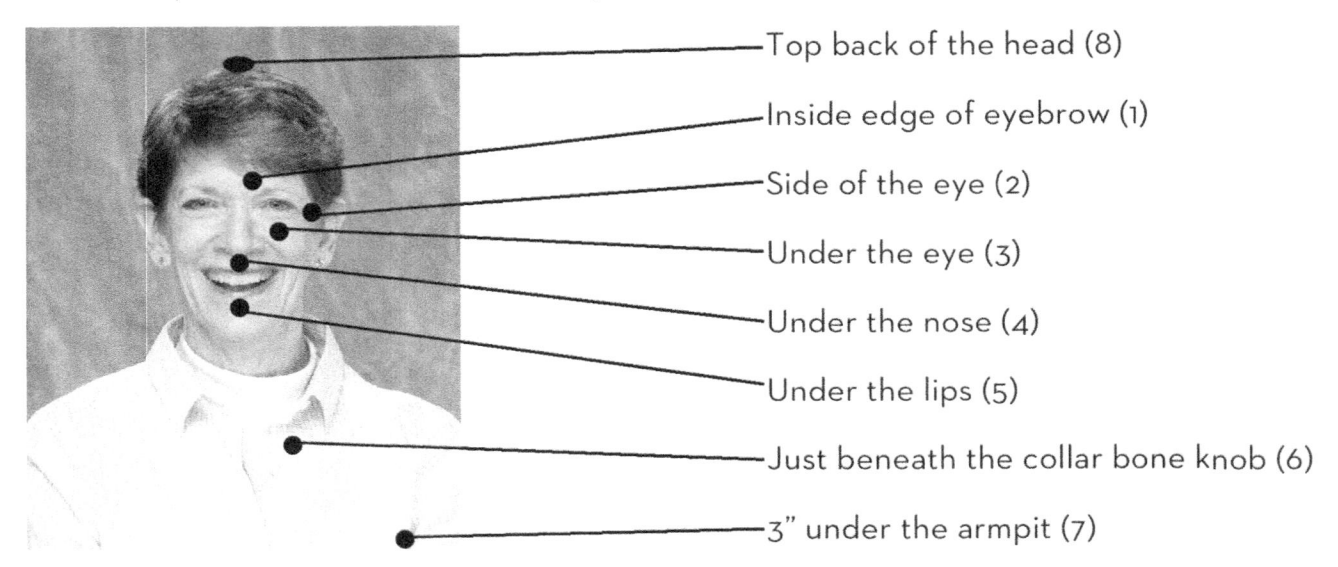

- Top back of the head (8)
- Inside edge of eyebrow (1)
- Side of the eye (2)
- Under the eye (3)
- Under the nose (4)
- Under the lips (5)
- Just beneath the collar bone knob (6)
- 3" under the armpit (7)

B. After tapping, take a deep breath. If you are not able to take a deep, full, satisfying breath, do eye rolls.

III. Eye rolls

A. With one hand tap continuously on the **back** of the other hand between the fourth and fifth fingers.
B. Hold your head straight forward, eyes looking straight down.
C. For six seconds, roll your eyes from the floor straight up toward the ceiling while repeating the tapping statement. Keep the head straight forward, only moving the eyes.

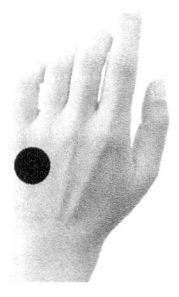

IV. Take another deep breath.

© Tessa Cason, 2022.

Chapter 8
EFT Tapping, Beliefs, and the Subconscious Mind

EFT – Emotional Freedom Technique

EFT is a technique that allows us to change dysfunctional beliefs and emotions on a subconscious level. It involves making a statement while tapping different points along meridian paths.

The general principle behind EFT is that the cause of all negative emotions is a disruption in the body's energy system. By tapping on locations where several different meridians flow, we can release unproductive memories, emotions, and beliefs that cause the blockages.

A Belief is...

A belief is a mental acceptance of, and conviction in, the Truth, actuality, or validity of something. It is what we believe to be true, whether it is Truth or not. A belief is a thought that influences energy all the time.

A Dysfunctional Belief is...

A dysfunctional belief is a belief that takes us away from peace, love, joy, stability, acceptance, and harmony. It causes us to feel stressed, fearful, anxious, and/or insecure.

The Conscious Mind is...

The conscious mind is the part of us that thinks, passes judgments, makes decisions, remembers, analyzes, has desires, and communicates with others. It is responsible for logic and reasoning, understanding and comprehension. The mind determines our actions, feelings, thoughts, judgments, and decisions **based on beliefs.**

The Subconscious Mind is...

The subconscious is the part of the mind responsible for all our involuntary actions like our heartbeat and breathing rate. It does not evaluate, make decisions, or pass judgment. It just is. It does not determine if something is "right" or "wrong."

The subconscious is much like the software of a computer. On the computer keyboard, if we press the key for the letter "a," we will see the letter "a" on the screen, even though we may have wanted to see "t." Just as a computer can only do what it has been programmed to do, we can only do as we are programmed to do.

© Tessa Cason, 2022.

Our programming is determined by our beliefs. Beliefs and memories are "stored" in the subconscious.

Three Rules of the Subconscious Mind

Three rules of the subconscious mind include:

1. Personal. It only understands "I," "me," "myself." First-person.

2. Positive. The subconscious does not hear the word "no." When you say, "I am not going to eat that piece of cake," the subconscious mind hears, "Yummm! Cake! I am going to eat a piece of that cake!"

3. Present time. Time does not exist for the subconscious. The only time it knows is "now," present time. "I'm going to start my diet tomorrow." "Tomorrow" never comes; thus, the diet never starts.

> Beliefs precede all of our thoughts, feelings,
> decisions, choices, actions, reactions,
> and experiences...
>
> Our beliefs and memories are stored
> in the subconscious mind.
>
> If we want to make changes in our lives,
> we have to change the programming,
> the dysfunctional beliefs in the subconscious.
>
> Three rules of the Subconscious Mind:
> Personal
> Positive
> Present time

© Tessa Cason, 2022.

Chapter 9
How Does EFT Tapping Work?

1. Acceptance: The last part of the tapping statement, we say, "I totally and completely accept myself." **Acceptance brings us into present time.** We can only heal if we are in present time.

2. Addresses the current dysfunctional beliefs on a subconscious level: To make changes in our lives, we have to change the dysfunctional beliefs on a subconscious level. The middle part of the tapping statements are the "instructions" for the subconscious. **To make changes in our lives, we only care what the subconscious hears.**

3. Pattern interrupt: Dysfunctional memories and/or beliefs block energy from flowing freely along the meridians. Tapping is a pattern interrupt that disrupts the flow of energy to allow our **body's own Infinite Wisdom to come forth for healing.** (Tapping both sides does not act as a pattern interrupt.)

4. Mis-direct: One role of the physical body is to protect us. When our hand is too close to a flame, our body automatically pulls our hand back to safety. An EFT Tapping statement that agrees with the current belief is more effective. The physical body is less likely to sabotage the tapping if it agrees with the current belief.

For the EFT Taping statement "I fear change":

* This statement appeases the physical body since it agrees with the current belief.
* The tapping disrupts the energy flow so our Truth can come forth.

> The body will always gravitate to health, wealth, and well-being when the conditions allow it. EFT Tapping weeds the garden so the blossoms can bloom more easily and effortlessly.

© Tessa Cason, 2022.

Chapter 10
Benefits of Using EFT Tapping

* The last part of the statement is, "I totally and completely **accept** myself." **Acceptance** brings us into present time. Healing can only take place when we are in present time.

* By tapping, we are **calling forth our Truths.** The keyword here is "**our.**" Not anyone else's. If my name is "Lucas," tapping the statement "Even though my name is Troy," my name will not change to Troy.

* Tapping **calls forth our body's Infinite Wisdom.** When we cut our finger, our body knows how to heal the cut itself. Once the dysfunctional emotions, experiences, and beliefs have been "deleted," our body **automatically** gravitates to health, wealth, wisdom, peace, love, joy...

* By changing dysfunctional beliefs and emotions on a subconscious level, the changes we make with EFT are **permanent.**

* EFT Tapping can change:
  Beliefs
  Emotions
  Self-images
  Our story
  Thoughts
  Mind chatter
  Painful memories

* EFT Tapping can neutralize stored memories that block energy along the meridians.

* EFT Tapping can desensitize emotions. We might have a difficult person in our life who ignores us and/or criticizes us, so we tap the statement: "This difficult person [or their name] ignores and criticizes me."

Tapping does not mean they will no longer ignore and/or criticize us; however, it can **desensitize us,** so we are no longer affected by their behavior. Once we have desensitized the emotions, our perception and mental thinking improve. We are better able to make informed decisions. We don't take and make everything personal. Our health is not negatively impacted. Our heart doesn't beat 100 beats/minute. Smoke stops coming out of our ears, and our faces don't turn red with anger and frustration.

© Tessa Cason, 2022.

Chapter 11
What We Say As We Tap Is VERY Important!

All of our beliefs are programmed into our subconscious minds. If we want to change our lives, we have to delete the dysfunctional beliefs on a subconscious level. The statements we make as we tap are the instructions for the subconscious mind.

THE TAPPING STATEMENTS WE WAY AS WE ARE TAPPING ARE CRITICAL FOR THIS TO HAPPEN!

Example: You get in a taxi. Several hours later, you still have not arrived at your destination. "*Why?*" you ask. Because you did not give the destination to the taxi driver!

Tapping without saying an adequate tapping statement is like riding in a cab without giving the cab driver our destination!

For EFT Tapping to be MOST EFFECTIVE the Tapping Statement is CRITICAL!

EFT Tapping allows us to delete the dysfunctional beliefs on a subconscious level. The statements we make as we tap are instructions to the subconscious mind so our Truth can come forth.

Chapter 12
Using a Negative EFT Tapping Statement

Our beliefs **precede** all of our thoughts, feelings, decisions, choices, actions, reactions, and experiences.

If we want to make changes in our lives, we have to change the dysfunctional beliefs. Our beliefs are stored in the subconscious.

To change our lives, to change a belief, we only care what the subconscious hears when we tap. The subconscious does not hear the word "no." When we say, "I am not going to eat that piece of cake," the subconscious hears, "Yummm, cake!"

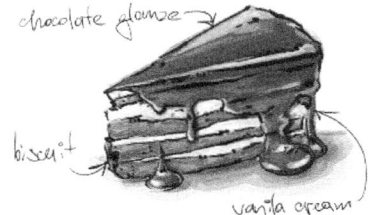

Example, if we don't believe we have what it takes to be successful and we tap the statement, "I have what it takes to be successful," the body could sabotage the tapping. We could tap and it won't clear.

Instead, if the statement we make is, "I do not have what it takes to be successful," the "**not**" appeases the physical body and the subconscious hears, "I have what it takes to be successful!"

A tapping statement with the word "no" or "not" works best!

© Tessa Cason, 2022.

Chapter 13
EFT Tapping Statements Are Most Effective When They Agree With Current Beliefs

The EFT Tapping statement is **more successful when** it **is something the body currently believes.**

> The body is less likely to sabotage an EFT Tapping statement that agrees with the current belief.

One role of the physical body is to protect us from harm. (For example, if our hand gets too close to a flame, our body will pull our hand back to safety.) The body is less likely to sabotage the statement and the process if the EFT Tapping statement agrees with the current belief. Thus, it appeases the physical body.

For example, if our desire is prosperity and wealth and we tap the statement, "I am prosperous now," the body could sabotage the tapping by forgetting what we were saying, getting easily distracted, or our mind chatter may remind us we are not prosperous. We could tap and the statement, most likely, will not clear.

If the statement we say is "I am not prosperous now," the "**not**" appeases the physical body, and the subconscious hears, "I am prosperous now!"

© Tessa Cason, 2022.

Chapter 14
The Very First EFT Tapping Statement to Tap

The very first EFT Tapping statement I have clients and students tap is, "It is not okay or safe for my life to change." I have muscle tested this statement with more than a thousand people. Not one person tested strong that it was okay or safe for their life to change. (Muscle testing is a way in which we can converse with the body, bypassing the conscious mind.)

How effective can EFT or any therapy be if it is not okay or safe for our lives to change?

Since our lives are constantly changing, if it is not okay or safe for our lives to change, every time our lives change, it creates stress for the body. Stress creates another whole set of issues for ourselves, our lives, and our bodies.

START — IT'S NOT OKAY OR SAFE FOR MY LIFE TO CHANGE.

© Tessa Cason, 2022.

Chapter 15
One Statement per Round of EFT vs Multiple Statements per Round of EFT

Laser-focused Tapping vs Round Robin Tapping

Same Statement for all the Tapping Points in One Round
vs Multiple Statements in One Round of Tapping (Scripts)

Two styles of tapping for different purposes. One style is best for healing dysfunctional beliefs. The other style is best for healing emotions, desensitizing a story, situation, and/or memory.

I found that the laser-focused, one statement for a round of tapping was most effective for healing the beliefs. Multiple statements per round of tapping is great at healing emotions, desensitizing a story, situation, and/or memory.

Same Statement for All the Tapping Points in One Round

After tapping the statement, "It's not okay for my life to change," and we are able to take a deep breath, we know the statement cleared. Then we tap, "I'm not ready for my life to change," and we are not able to take a deep breath, most likely, the statement did not clear.

Knowing the statement did not clear, we can focus on the reasons, excuses, and/or beliefs about not being ready to change our lives.

* Maybe the changes we need to make would require more of us than we want to give.
* Maybe we don't feel we have the abilities we would need if our life changed.
* Maybe we don't feel our support system, the people in our life, would support the changes we want to make.

Follow-up tapping statements for "I'm not ready for my life to change" could be:

* I do not have the abilities change would require.
* I am afraid of change.
* Others will not support the changes I want to make in my life.
* I am not able to make the changes I want to make.
* I do not have the courage that change would require.
* I am too old to change.

© Tessa Cason, 2022.

Tapping the same statement at all eight points is most effective for clearing beliefs. When a statement does not clear, we can focus on the reasons, excuses, and/or dysfunctional beliefs that blocked the statement from clearing.

Multiple Statements in One Round of Tapping (Scripts/Round Robin)

Tapping multiple statements in one round, also known as Scripts or Round Robin tapping, is excellent for healing a story, and desensitizing a memory or story.

Healing a broken heart, to desensitize the heartache of the break up, the following script/statements could be said, one statement/point:

* My boyfriend broke up with me.
* I am heartbroken.
* He said he doesn't love me anymore.
* I do not know how I can go on without him.
* It hurts.
* I am sad he doesn't love me anymore.
* I am sad our relationship is over.
* I will never find anyone like him ever again.

Reframing:

Reframing is a Neuro Linguistic Programming (NLP) term. It is a way to view and experience emotions, situations, and/or behaviors in a more positive manner.

At the end of round robin tapping, we can introduce statements to "reframe" the situation.

An example of reframing could be:

* I want this chocolate.
* Maybe eating chocolate is wanting to reconnect to my childhood.
* Maybe eating sugar is a way of being loved.
* Maybe I can find a different way of being loved.

Round robin tapping, scripts, can desensitize the hurt and pain. It can heal the pain of our story. It may not rewrite the beliefs. To clear out the beliefs, it would be necessary to look at the reasons the relationship didn't work and why our heart is broken, or why we crave chocolate.

Round robin/script tapping can also be done by just tapping the side of the hand.

© Tessa Cason, 2022.

Side of Hand Tapping to Desensitize a Story, Situation, and/or Memory

Just as in the round robin tapping/scripts, we said different statements, one after the other, we can say the same statements and just tap the side of the hand.

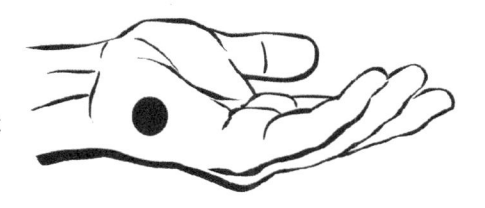

If a memory still "haunts" us, embarrasses us, and/or affects our actions in any way, this technique might be perfect to neutralize the memory.

For example:

As Sasha remembers the first dance she attended as a teen-ager, tears well up in her eyes. She starts to tap the side of the hand (SOH) as she tells her story:

My best friend, Samantha and I, were so excited about attending our first high school dance. We weren't old enough to drive so Sam's dad dropped us off in front of the high school auditorium where the dance was held.

(Continue to tap the SOH) We were in awe of how the auditorium was transformed into a palace. Sofas were placed around a hardwood dance floor in the center of the room. We promised each other we would be there for the other throughout the night so neither of us would be stranded alone.

(Continue to tap the SOH) Well, along came Billy McDaniels. Sam had had a crush on Billy since third grade. He asked her to dance and I never saw her again for the rest of the night.

(Continue to tap the SOH) Those three hours were probably the worst night of my entire life! No one asked me to dance. Every time I joined a group of girls, a new song would begin, and every one of them was asked to dance, everyone except me. I don't know why no one asked me to dance. I felt ugly, abandoned, and undesirable! Talk about being a wallflower. I thought I was invisible. I wanted to hide from embarrassment.

(Continue to tap the SOH) This was back in the days before cell phones. The auditorium didn't have a payphone to call my parents to come and get me. I had to endure three hours of humiliation watching every single girl be asked to dance EXCEPT me.

(Continue to tap the SOH) I never attended another high school dance again!

Whether we tap the side of the hand or the eight tapping points, the result is the same. Round robin tapping can desensitize emotions and memories very effectively.

There are different styles of EFT Tapping.
Find the style that works best for your desired result.

© Tessa Cason, 2022.

Chapter 16
Walking Backwards EFT (Backing Up)

As I was working with a client, they had an issue that was not clearing. Knowing that movement helps to clear issues, I decided to have the person stand up and walk backward. Literally, walk backward, step after step, facing forward while their feet moved backward.

Surprise, surprise, it worked. Every statement cleared as she backed up.

The next client came in. I had him walk backwards, and it worked with clearing issues for him as well. Both clients were somewhat athletic and did workout. I wanted to know if the Backing Up would work with non-athletic people. I was teaching an EFT class the next day. At the end of the class, we all backed up together. And, IT WORKED!

Let's say we want to process, "I will never be comfortable in the world." Stand up. Make sure nothing is behind you. Then walk backward while facing forward and say, "I will never be comfortable in the world. I will never be comfortable in the world. I will never be comfortable in the world. I will never be comfortable in the world." Repeat the phrase six - eight times.

When we back up, we say the same statement we would have made if we were tapping. We don't have to say the "Even though" or the last remainder phrase, "I totally and completely accept myself."

> Walking forward represents forward movement in our lives. Walking backward represents the past.
>
> Physical movement can help clear emotional issues and facilitate change.
>
> Walking backward undoes the past and helps to clear, heal, and transform an issue in our lives.

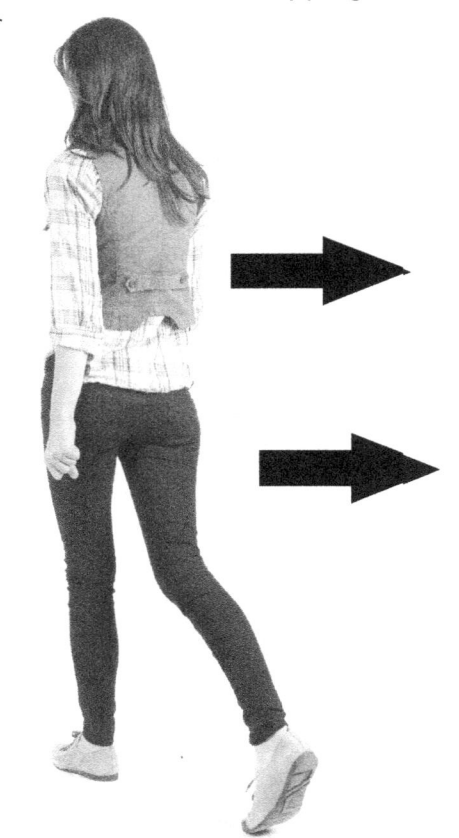

© Tessa Cason, 2022.

Chapter 17
Intensity Level

One measure of knowing how much an issue has been resolved is to begin, before tapping, by giving the issue an intensity number (IL) between 1 and 10, with 10 being high.

For example, we want a romantic partnership, yet we haven't met "the one." Thinking about a romantic relationship happening, what is the likelihood, on a scale of 1 – 10, with 10 being very likely and 1, not likely at all, of a romantic relationship happening?

Okay. We give ourselves a 2. Now, let's start tapping!

When asked what the issues might be, "Well," we say, "it does not seem as if the people who I want, want me."

Great tapping statement. Tap, "Even though the people I want don't want me, I totally and completely accept myself." After tapping, we check in with ourselves; the IL has gone up to a 4, so it is now a little bit more likely.

What comes to mind now? "No one will find me desirable." Great tapping statement. "Even though no one will find me desirable, I totally and completely accept myself." Check the IL. How likely? 5. Cool! Progress.

What comes to mind now? "I'm not comfortable being vulnerable in romantic relationships." Great tapping statement. "Even though I'm not comfortable being vulnerable in a romantic relationship, I totally and completely accept myself." Check the IL. Now it is a 6. Still progress.

What comes to mind now? "Well, it feels like if I am in a relationship, I will lose a lot of my freedom." Make this into a tapping statement. "Even though I will lose my freedom when I am in a relationship, I totally and completely accept myself." The IL has gone up to a 7.

What comes to mind now? "Oh, if I was in a relationship, I would have to be accountable to someone!" Make this into a tapping statement: "Even though, I would have to be accountable to someone if I was in a relationship, I totally and completely accept myself." Wow...the IL is 9, very likely!

Giving an issue an Intensity Level gives at the beginning and throughout the session gives us an indication of the progress we are making with resolving and/or healing that issue in our lives.

© Tessa Cason, 2022.

Chapter 18
Yawning and Taking a Deep Breath

From Traditional Chinese Medicine, we know that when chi (energy) flows freely through the meridians, the body is healthy and balanced. Physical, mental, and/or emotional illness can result when the energy is blocked.

Dysfunctional beliefs and emotions produce blocks along the meridians, blocking energy from flowing freely in the body.

With EFT Tapping, as we tap, we release the blocks. As blocked energy is able to flow more freely, the body can now "breathe a sigh of relief." Yawning is that sigh of relief.

If, after tapping, we can take a complete, deep, full, and satisfying breath, we know that an EFT Tapping statement has cleared. This yawn is an indication that an EFT Tapping statement has cleared.

If the yawn or breath is not a full, deep breath then the statement did not clear completely.

Chapter 19
Integration...What Happens After Tapping

After tapping, our system needs some downtime for integration to take place. When the physical body and the mind are "idle," integration can take place.

Sometimes, in the first 24 hours after tapping, we might find ourselves vegging more than normal, sleeping more than normal, or more tired than normal. This downtime is needed to integrate the new changes.

After installing a new program into our computer, sometimes we have to reboot the computer (shut down and restart) for the new program to be integrated into the system.

After tapping, our bodies need to reboot. We need some downtime. When we sleep, the new changes are integrated.

> HEALING BEGINS NATURALLY AFTER THE BODY HAS HAD A CHANCE TO INTEGRATE.

Sometimes, after tapping, we forget the intensity of our pain and think that feeling better had nothing to do with tapping. Something so simple could not possibly create the improvement in our state of mind!

When we cut our finger, once it is healed, we don't even remember cutting our finger. As we move toward health, wealth, and well-being, sometimes we don't remember how unhappy, restless, or isolated we once felt.

© Tessa Cason, 2022.

Chapter 20
EFT Tapping Doesn't Work for Me

Why might EFT Tapping not be working?

* The tapping statement might not be worded such that a dysfunctional belief and/or emotion is addressed and eliminated.
* The style (laser-focused style vs round robin) of tapping may not be effective for the statement to be cleared.
* The EFT Tapping statement is only addressing a symptom and **not the cause of the issue.**

FOR EFT TAPPING TO BE EFFECTIVE, THE CAUSE OF THE ISSUE NEEDS TO BE HEALED.

* Having an awareness of our issues does not heal the dysfunctional beliefs.
* Forgiving ourselves and/or someone else does not heal the dysfunctional beliefs.
* Talk therapy does not heal the dysfunctional beliefs.
* Desensitizing the emotions does not heal the dysfunctional beliefs.
* Healing the experience of a hurtful event does not change the dysfunctional beliefs.

EFT Tapping works best when

1) the statements are worded to eliminate the dysfunctional beliefs,
2) the most effective style of tapping is utilized, and
3) we are healing the cause, not just the symptoms.

Chapter 21
What to Do if an EFT Tapping Statement Does Not Clear

When a statement might not clear, turn the statement into a question. The statement, "It's not okay for me to be powerful," didn't clear. **Turn the tapping statement into a question:** "Why isn't it okay for me to be powerful?"

The answer might be:

* Powerful people are ruthless and heartless.
* I am afraid of being powerful.
* Being powerful would change me for the worse.
* Power corrupts.
* People would laugh at me if I tried being powerful.
* I would have to give up my fears and anxieties to be powerful.
* I might be called aggressive if I tried being powerful.
* I do not have the abilities, skills, or qualities to be powerful.
* Others would make fun of me if I tried being powerful.
* Powerful people are thoughtless and self-centered.

With these beliefs, it might not be okay or safe to be powerful or even explore the idea of being powerful. The statements above are tapping statements. Tap the answer to the question.

After tapping the answer to the question, revisit the original statement that did not clear. Most likely, it will now be cleared, and you will be able to take a full, deep, and complete breath.

Chapter 22
Science and EFT Tapping Research

EFT has been researched in more than ten countries by more than sixty investigators whose results have been published in more than twenty different peer-reviewed journals. Two leading researchers are Dawson Church, Ph.D. and David Feinstein, Ph.D.

Dr. Dawson Church, a leading expert on energy psychology and an EFT master, has gathered all the research information, and it can be found on this website: www.EFTUniverse.com.

Two Research Studies

1) Harvard Medical School Studies and the Brain's Stress Response

Studies at the Harvard Medical School reveal that stimulating the body's meridian points significantly reduces activity in a part of the brain called the amygdala.

The amygdala can be thought of as the body's alarm system. When the body is experiencing trauma or fear, the amygdala is triggered, and the body is flooded with cortisol, also known as the stress hormone. The stress response sets up an intricate chain reaction.

The studies showed that stimulating or tapping points along the meridians such as EFT Tapping, drastically reduced and/or eliminated the stress response and the resulting chain reaction.

2) Dr. Dawson Church and Cortisol Reduction

Another significant study was conducted by Dr. Dawson Church. He studied the impact an hour's tapping session had on the cortisol levels of eighty-three subjects. He also measured the cortisol levels of people who received traditional talk therapy and those of a third group who received no treatment at all.

On average, for the eighty-three subjects who completed an hour tapping session, cortisol levels were reduced by 24%. Some subjects experienced a 50% reduction in cortisol levels.

The subjects who completed one hour of traditional talk therapy and those who had completed neither session did not experience any significant cortisol reduction.

Chapter 23
Is Lowering the Cortisol Level Enough to Permanently Change Our Lives?

Several things can lower our cortisol (stress hormone) levels including:
* Power posing
* Meditating
* Laughing
* Exercising regularly
* Listening to music
* Getting a massage
* Eliminating caffeine from our diet
* Eating a balanced, nutritious meal and eliminating processed food

Would performing any of the above activities lower our cortisol level enough to permanently change our lives? Only if the activity eliminates the dysfunctional beliefs on a subconscious level.

All of our thoughts, feelings, actions, reactions, choices, and decisions are preceded by a belief. To change our lives, the dysfunctional beliefs must be eliminated.

Power posing, listening to music, or eating a balanced meal will not permanently change our lives. Exercising will help our physical body but will not delete our dysfunctional beliefs. Laughing will bring us into the present so we will not be drawn into our fears or anger, but it will not change our lives. Meditating helps us to center and balance, but will not change our lives on a permanent basis.

To change our lives, we must be able to recognize, acknowledge, and take ownership of that which we want to change then delete the dysfunctional emotions and beliefs that preceded that what we want to change on a subconscious level.

> EFT Tapping will delete dysfunctional emotions and beliefs on a subconscious level if we provide the correct "instructions" to our subconscious mind. We must word the tapping statements in the subconscious' language. We must word the tapping statement so the subconscious mind hears what we want to eliminate.

© Tessa Cason, 2022.

Chapter 24
Tapping Affirmations

* I am healthy and happy.
* Wealth is pouring into my life.
* I radiate love and happiness.
* I have the perfect job for me.
* I am successful in whatever I do.

If we were to tap "I am healthy and happy now" and we are not, most likely, as we are tapping, we might think, "Yeah, right. Sure. I am healthy and happy. My life sucks. I hate my job. I am always broke. There is never enough money…"

The body knows this is not true. We are not healthy and happy now. When we tap, we might have difficulty remembering what we are saying, lose focus and concentration, and/or the mind drifts.

An EFT Tapping statement is most effective **when** it matches our current belief.

The subconscious does not hear the word "No." One way of tapping affirmations and, at the same time, putting in the positives is to put the word "no" into the tapping statements.

* I am **not** healthy and happy. Subconscious hears: I am healthy and happy.
* Wealth is **not** pouring into my life. Subconscious hears: Wealth is pouring into my life.
* I **do not** radiate love and happiness. Subconscious hears: I radiate love and happiness.
* I **do not** have the perfect job for me. Subconscious hears: I have the perfect job for me.
* I am **not** successful in whatever I do. Subconscious hears: I am successful in whatever I do.

If we repeat affirmations over and over and over before we clear the affirmation with EFT Tapping, repeating the affirmation numerous times will have little effect except to create circumstances in our lives so we can be confronted with the beliefs that do not align with the affirmation.

© Tessa Cason, 2022.

Chapter 25
Finishing Touches (Optional)

relax

Some like to finish their tapping with statements that are centering and calming. If this is you, then you might want to try the 16 statements on the next page or make up those that you like. The statements can be said in any order that works for you.

Tapping Location	Statement
Eyebrow	All is well in my life.
Temple	Every day in every way I am getting better and better.
Under the Eye	I am fulfilled in every way, every day.
Under the Nose	My blessings appears in rich appropriate form with divine timing.
Under the Lips	I am an excellent steward of wealth and am blessed with great abundance.
Under the Collarbone Knob	I take complete responsibility for everything in my life.
Under the Arm	I have all the tools, skills, and abilities to excel in my life.
Top back part of the Head	I know I will be able to handle anything that arises in my life.
Eyebrow	All my dreams, hopes, wishes, and goals are being fulfilled each and every day.
Temple	Divine love expressing through me, now draws to me new ideas.
Under the Eye	I am comfortable with my life changing.
Under the Nose	I am able to create all that I desire.
Under the Lips	I know what needs to be done and follow through to completion.
Under the Collarbone Knob	My health is perfect in every way, physically, mentally, emotionally, and spiritually.
Under the Arm	I invite into my subconscious Archangel Raphael to heal all that needs to be forgiven, released, and redeemed. Cleanse me and free me from it now.
Top back part of the Head	The light of God surrounds me. The love of God enfolds me. The power of God protects me. The

Chapter 26
How to Use This Book

1. The statements are divided into sections. Read through the statements in one section. As you read a statement, notice if you have any reaction to the statement or feel the statement might be true for you. If so, note the number for that statement.

2. Once you have completed reading all the statements in one section, go back and reread the statements you noted and rate them on a scale of 1 – 10, with 10 being a "biggie."

3. List the top statements.

4. From this list, select one and describe how it plays out in your life. It is important to recognize and identify the pattern. What are the consequences of having this belief? Is there a trigger? How does it begin? How does it benefit you? How has it harmed you? There will be a different example listed in each section.

5. Tap the statements. Statements can be combined for scripts…a different statement on each of the different tapping points in one round of tapping.

6. Describe any flashbacks or memories that you might have had as you were tapping out the statements. Describe any ah-has, insights, and/or thoughts you might have had as a result of tapping the statements.

7. After tapping all the statements, review them to determine if you still have a reaction to any of the statements. If you do, you have several options. One, put a "Why" before the statement. Tap out the answer. Secondly, note that this statement may not have cleared and continue on to the next section. Most likely, after additional statements are tapped, statements that may not have cleared, will clear without having to tap the statement again.

8. Allow some downtime for integration and for the body to heal.

9. The number of sections you do at a time will be up to you. Initially, you might want to do one section to determine if you get tired and need to have some downtime after tapping.

10. The day after tapping, again review the statements you tapped to determine if you still have a reaction. If you do, follow the instructions in #7.

© Tessa Cason, 2022.

1 – 20 EFT Tapping Statements

*Have the courage to follow your heart and intuition.
They somehow already know what you truly want to become.*

Steve Jobs

1. Intuition is evil.
2. I am not intuitive.
3. I let fear stop me.
4. I ignore my hunches.
5. Channeling is an act.
6. Intuition is not a skill.
7. Intuition is not logical.
8. I don't follow my heart.
9. I ignore my inner voice.
10. Trusting intuition is evil.
11. I don't trust my intuition.
12. I am not a spiritual being.
13. No one I know is intuitive.
14. I don't honor my intuition.
15. Being intuitive is too hard.
16. I'm not good at visualizing.
17. I can't learn to be intuitive.
18. Only women have intuition.
19. Intuition serves no purpose.
20. I'm not sure what a hunch is.

Journaling Pages for Statements 1 – 20

I would love it if the information came in like a telegram. But, that isn't how it happens. Instead, the information arrives in shorthand.

Echo Bodine

1. From the tapping statements between 1 – 20, list the top seven statements that you thought or felt applied to you:

1.

2.

3.

4.

5.

6.

7.

2. From this list of seven statements, select one and describe how it plays out in your life. Give an example or two. It is important to recognize and identify the pattern. Is there a trigger? How does it begin? How has it benefited you? How has it harmed you? For instance, do you believe that intuition is something you have or don't have that it's not a skill? Is this a reason not to be intuitive or do you believe you don't have what it takes to learn a new skill?

3. Tap out the top 7 statements.

4. As you were tapping out the statements, did you have any flashback or memories of the past, any additional insights, and/or ah-ha thoughts? If so, write them down. Make note of them.

21 – 40 EFT Tapping Statements

Intuition will tell the thinking mind where to look next.

Jonas Salk

21. My intuition is not to be trusted.
22. Logic is the sole guide in my life.
23. I don't want to trust my intuition.
24. Hunches have no value in my life.
25. Intuitive insights are not realistic.
26. People are either intuitive or not.
27. Intuition is too mysterious for me.
28. Being intuitive is too complicated.
29. I smell things that are not present.
30. I'm not aware of what I am feeling.
31. I'm not aware of my intuitive "hits."
32. I don't believe that intuition works.
33. Intuition knows, instantly, in a flash.
34. I'm not wise enough to be intuitive.
35. I don't know how to protect myself.
36. I'm not quiet enough to be intuitive.
37. Practicing will not develop intuition.
38. I worry when I just know something.
39. I don't receive intuitive information.
40. Intuition is synonymous with trance.

Journaling Pages for Statements 21 – 40

Intuition is the innate ability in everyone to perceive truth directly, not by reason, logic, or analysis, but by a simple knowing from within. This is the very meaning of the word "intuition": to know or understand from within from one's own self and from the heart. Intuition is the inner ability to see behind the outer forms of things to their inner essence.

J. Donald Walters

1. From the tapping statements between 1 – 20, list the top seven statements that you thought or felt applied to you:

1.

2.

3.

4.

5.

6.

7.

2. From this list of seven statements, select one and describe how it plays out in your life. Give an example or two. It is important to recognize and identify the pattern. Is there a trigger? How does it begin? How has it benefited you? How has it harmed you? For instance, do you think you don't receive guidance every time you ask? Would you recognize the answer if the answer was something different than what you wanted to hear?

3. Tap out the top 7 statements.

4. As you were tapping out the statements, did you have any flashback or memories of the past, any additional insights, and/or ah-ha thoughts? If so, write them down. Make note of them.

© Tessa Cason, 2022.

41 – 60 EFT Tapping Statements

Intuition doesn't tell you what you want to hear; it tells you what you need to hear.
Sonia Choquette

41. I will lose me if I am intuitive.
42. No one I know uses intuition.
43. Intuition has no value for me.
44. I'm too fearful to be intuitive.
45. Intuition doesn't make sense.
46. I'm too logical to be intuitive.
47. Intuition is the work of Satan.
48. I ignore the gut feelings I get.
49. I am not willing to be intuitive.
50. Trusting inner guidance is evil.
51. Intuition does not work for me.
52. I soak up everyone else's vibes.
53. I look to others for my answers.
54. I'm too skeptical to be intuitive.
55. I am too rational to be intuitive.
56. I complicate my interpretations.
57. Being intuitive is overwhelming.
58. I forget to listen to my intuition.
59. Claiming to be psychic is an act.
60. Intuition is the work of the devil.

Journaling Pages for Statements 41 – 60

Intuition involves more than simply 'going with your gut' or 'trusting your hunches'. A common misconception about intuition is that it means not having to thinks about things. Even the expression 'going with your gut' implies that intuition does not take place in your head.

Laura Day

1. From the tapping statements between 1 – 20, list the top seven statements that you thought or felt applied to you:

1.

2.

3.

4.

5.

6.

7.

2. From this list of seven statements, select one and describe how it plays out in your life. Give an example or two. It is important to recognize and identify the pattern. Is there a trigger? How does it begin? How has it benefited you? How has it harmed you? For instance, do you believe intuition is supposed to make sense? Is this the logical mind or the part of you that doesn't understand your intuition's language?

3. Tap out the top 7 statements.

4. As you were tapping out the statements, did you have any flashback or memories of the past, any additional insights, and/or ah-ha thoughts? If so, write them down. Make note of them.

61 – 80 EFT Tapping Statements

Intuition is a spiritual faculty. It does not explain, but simply points the way.

Florence Scovel Shinn

61. I care too much to be a good psychic.
62. Serendipity has no meaning in my life.
63. I might be wrong in my interpretation.
64. My gut feelings don't make any sense.
65. The only voice I hear within is my own.
66. Intuitive insights are just make believe.
67. Intuition is too subtle for me to sense.
68. I'm not relaxed enough to be intuitive.
69. Intuition is synonymous with hypnosis.
70. Following my intuition is not practical.
71. My logic challenges my intuitive "hits."
72. I don't respect the guidance I receive.
73. I only rely on logic and common sense.
74. I might be wrong if I try to be intuitive.
75. I'm not spiritual enough to be intuitive.
76. I don't know how to trust my guidance.
77. Inner guidance is the work of the devil.
78. Intuition is synonymous with witchcraft.
79. I'm not sensitive enough to be intuitive.
80. Intuition is nothing more than guessing.

© Tessa Cason, 2022.

Journaling Pages for Statements 61 - 80

The intellect has little to do on the road to discovery. There comes a leap in consciousness, call it intuition or what you will, and the solution comes to you and you don't know why or how.

Albert Einstein

1. From the tapping statements between 1 – 20, list the top seven statements that you thought or felt applied to you:

1.

2.

3.

4.

5.

6.

7.

2. From this list of seven statements, select one and describe how it plays out in your life. Give an example or two. It is important to recognize and identify the pattern. Is there a trigger? How does it begin? How has it benefited you? How has it harmed you? For instance, might you be wrong if you tried to be intuitive? Maybe. Until you learn the skill. Being wrong, does that stop you from doing other things as well or just being intuitive?

3. Tap out the top 7 statements.

4. As you were tapping out the statements, did you have any flashback or memories of the past, any additional insights, and/or ah-ha thoughts? If so, write them down. Make note of them.

© Tessa Cason, 2022.

81 – 100 EFT Tapping Statements

Intuition is a heart message minus the static.
Sue Patton Thoele

81. No one I know values their intuition.
82. Intuitive hunches are unpredictable.
83. I'm not aware enough to be intuitive.
84. I'm not committed to being intuitive.
85. Women are more intuitive than men.
86. I am not willing to trust my intuition.
87. I'm too fearful to follow my intuition.
88. I don't know how to follow my heart.
89. I don't honor the guidance I receive.
90. My intuition must prove itself to me.
91. I don't honor or respect my intuition.
92. I don't respect my intuitive impulses.
93. God does not want us to be intuitive.
94. Being intuitive will lead to heartache.
95. Intuitive is synonymous with weirdos.
96. I don't know how I know what I know.
97. I don't have the ability to be intuitive.
98. There is not truth in intuitive insights.
99. I must rely on God for all my answers.
100. I don't have access to all the answers.

© Tessa Cason, 2022.

Journaling Pages for Statements 81 – 100

For the spiritual being, intuition is far more than a hunch. It is viewed as Guidance or as God talking, and this inner insight is never taken lightly or ignored.

Wayne Dyer

1. From the tapping statements between 1 – 20, list the top seven statements that you thought or felt applied to you:

1.

2.

3.

4.

5.

6.

7.

2. From this list of seven statements, select one and describe how it plays out in your life. Give an example or two. It is important to recognize and identify the pattern. Is there a trigger? How does it begin? How has it benefited you? How has it harmed you? For instance, does your intuition have to prove itself to you? Intuition is a skill. If you haven't developed the skill, how can it prove itself to you?

3. Tap out the top 7 statements.

4. As you were tapping out the statements, did you have any flashback or memories of the past, any additional insights, and/or ah-ha thoughts? If so, write them down. Make note of them.

© Tessa Cason, 2022.

101 – 120 EFT Tapping Statements

Our intuition is our inner GPS – Global Positioning System.
Tessa Cason

101. I'm not committed to acting on my intuition.
102. I don't believe in guides or guardian angels.
103. I don't accept my extrasensory impressions.
104. The impressions I receive must make sense.
105. I don't know how to practice being intuitive.
106. My anger gets in the way of being intuitive.
107. I don't know how to listen to my inner voice.
108. I'm not open-minded enough to be intuitive.
109. I don't understand the language of symbols.
110. I'm not right-brained enough to be intuitive.
111. Intuition is not a skill that can be developed.
112. Intuition is nothing more than lucky guesses.
113. I can't trust my intuition for decision-making.
114. I cannot see/hear/feel intuitive information.
115. Nothing good can come from being intuitive.
116. Others are threatened by my being intuitive.
117. I would look stupid if my intuition was wrong.
118. I don't know how to learn to use my intuition.
119. It's not okay/safe for me to trust my intuition.
120. The messages I receive are always confusing.

© Tessa Cason, 2022.

Journaling Pages for Statements 101 – 120

Intellect is the functioning of the head, instinct is the functioning of your body, and intuition is the functioning of your heart. And behind these three is your being, whose only quality is witnessing.

Osho

1. From the tapping statements between 1 – 20, list the top seven statements that you thought or felt applied to you:

1.

2.

3.

4.

5.

6.

7.

2. From this list of seven statements, select one and describe how it plays out in your life. Give an example or two. It is important to recognize and identify the pattern. Is there a trigger? How does it begin? How has it benefited you? How has it harmed you? For instance, are the messages you receive confusing? Have you learned the language of your intuition? As with any skill, it takes practice, practice, and more practice.

3. Tap out the top 7 statements.

4. As you were tapping out the statements, did you have any flashback or memories of the past, any additional insights, and/or ah-ha thoughts? If so, write them down. Make note of them.

121 – 140 EFT Tapping Statements

*Good instincts usually tell you what to do
before your head has figured it out.*

Michael Burke

121. I don't know how to access my intuition.
122. Listening to my intuition is not practical.
123. There is no significance to coincidences.
124. It is silly to think that I could be intuitive.
125. I'm not reflective enough to be intuitive.
126. It is not okay/safe for me to be intuitive.
127. I'm not open to my intuitive impressions.
128. Intuition is only available to a gifted few.
129. Intuitive information is not to be trusted.
130. I'm not willing to practice being intuitive.
131. Intuition is unreliable and untrustworthy.
132. I'm afraid to develop my psychic abilities.
133. I don't receive guidance every time I ask.
134. I'm not committed to my spiritual growth.
135. Intuition is not meant to be of assistance.
136. I don't listen to the signals from my body.
137. It's too big of a risk to follow my intuition.
138. Intuition is too mysterious to understand.
139. I'm not in my body enough to be intuitive.
140. I'm not perceptive enough to be intuitive.

© Tessa Cason, 2022.

Journaling Pages for Statements 121 - 140

The intuitive mind is a sacred gift and the rational mind is a faithful servant. We have created a society that honors the servant and has forgotten the gift.

Albert Einstein

1. From the tapping statements between 1 - 20, list the top seven statements that you thought or felt applied to you:

1.

2.

3.

4.

5.

6.

7.

2. From this list of seven statements, select one and describe how it plays out in your life. Give an example or two. It is important to recognize and identify the pattern. Is there a trigger? How does it begin? How has it benefited you? How has it harmed you? For instance, do you believe that intuition is only available to a few gifted individuals? If so, how would you define hunches, or gut feelings, or a "mother's intuition?"

3. Tap out the top 7 statements.

4. As you were tapping out the statements, did you have any flashback or memories of the past, any additional insights, and/or ah-ha thoughts? If so, write them down. Make note of them.

141 – 160 EFT Tapping Statements

A person uses their intelligence to find reasons to support their intuition.
G. K. Chesterton

141. I don't want others to know I am intuitive.
142. I lack the skill to learn how to be intuitive.
143. My inner voice sounds like my inner critic.
144. Following my intuition might be a mistake.
145. My mind isn't clear enough to be intuitive.
146. I dismiss my gut feelings as unworthy info.
147. Reasoning is more accurate than intuition.
148. Others will think me weird if I am intuitive.
149. I'm not committed to trusting my intuition.
150. Intuition is nothing more than imagination.
151. The dead don't talk to us from their grave.
152. Being intuitive might make me look stupid.
153. I will be disappointed if I trust my intuition.
154. Intuition is synonymous with casting spells.
155. I will be disappointed if I try to be intuitive.
156. Listening to my intuition is self-destructive.
157. I'm going straight to hell for being intuitive.
158. I'm not committed to honoring my intuition.
159. It's too hard to figure out what I am feeling.
160. I don't trust the accuracy of my perception.

© Tessa Cason, 2022.

Journaling Pages for Statements 141 – 160

When we listen to our intuition it connects us with a great knowledge, that part of us with an overview of our life that has our best interest at heart. It can provide an oasis of peace in the midst of chaos, bring us to harmony, help us release judgements, and give us confidence to take action and prepare for change in our life.

Lynn Robinson

1. From the tapping statements between 1 – 20, list the top seven statements that you thought or felt applied to you:

1.

2.

3.

4.

5.

6.

7.

2. From this list of seven statements, select one and describe how it plays out in your life. Give an example or two. It is important to recognize and identify the pattern. Is there a trigger? How does it begin? How has it benefited you? How has it harmed you? For instance, is intuition nothing more than an active imagination? Maybe. It helps to be imaginative when it comes to being intuitive. Having an imagination helps to interpret the language of your intuition.

3. Tap out the top 7 statements.

4. As you were tapping out the statements, did you have any flashback or memories of the past, any additional insights, and/or ah-ha thoughts? If so, write them down. Make note of them.

161 – 180 EFT Tapping Statements

*When you reach the end of what you should know,
you will be at the beginning of what you should sense.*

Kahlil Gibrán

161. Being intuitive would set me apart from others.
162. Self doubt gets in the way of my being intuitive.
163. I don't know how to interpret the hunches I get.
164. I'm uncertain if my intuition is guiding me or not.
165. I don't understand the language of the Universe.
166. I want a guarantee before acting on my intuition.
167. Intuition is not an information gathering process.
168. My logical mind censors my intuitive impressions.
169. I don't know how to integrate intuition with logic.
170. I must figure everything out with my logical mind.
171. I don't know which thoughts are intuitive insights.
172. It's not possible to correctly just know something.
173. I can't tell if it's their stuff or my stuff I am feeling.
174. My mind is full of too much chatter to be intuitive.
175. I can't distinguish between thoughts and intuition.
176. I value other people's opinions more than my own.
177. I'm too embarrassed to tell anyone of my hunches.
178. I will be punished when I follow my inner guidance.
179. My thinking mind interferes with my intuitive mind.
180. I ignore and discount my gut feelings and hunches.

© Tessa Cason, 2022.

Journaling Pages for Statements 161 - 180

Come from the heart, the true heart, not the head. When in doubt, choose the heart. This does not mean to deny your own experiences and that which you have empirically learned through the years. It means to trust your self to integrate intuition and experience. There is a balance, a harmony to be nurtured, between the head and the heart. When the intuition rings clear and true, loving impulses are favored.

Brian Weiss

1. From the tapping statements between 1 – 20, list the top seven statements that you thought or felt applied to you:

1.

2.

3.

4.

5.

6.

7.

2. From this list of seven statements, select one and describe how it plays out in your life. Give an example or two. It is important to recognize and identify the pattern. Is there a trigger? How does it begin? How has it benefited you? How has it harmed you? For instance, does your thinking mind interfere with your intuitive mind? Does everything have to be logical and planned out? And what of spontaneity and anything that is unplanned? Are they ignored? Are you ignoring your intuition?

3. Tap out the top 7 statements.

4. As you were tapping out the statements, did you have any flashback or memories of the past, any additional insights, and/or ah-ha thoughts? If so, write them down. Make note of them.

© Tessa Cason, 2022.

181 – 200 EFT Tapping Statements

It is by logic and science that we prove,
but by intuition that we discover.

Jules Henri Poincaré

181. Intuition is nothing more than common sense.
182. There is no significance to the things I notice.
183. I'm not committed to listening to my intuition.
184. I'm not in present time enough to be intuitive.
185. I don't get an answer when I ask for guidance.
186. I cloud my intuition with knowledge and logic.
187. My experience of the world must make sense.
188. Listening to my intuition would not be helpful.
189. I don't dare tell anyone about my gut feelings.
190. It's not safe for me to trust my inner guidance.
191. I don't allow intuitive meanings to come to me.
192. My logical mind interferes with being intuitive.
193. I'm not grounded enough to trust my intuition.
194. Intuition is nothing more than wishful thinking.
195. It's not okay/safe for me to follow my intuition.
196. My family would ridicule me for being intuitive.
197. I don't know how to practice at being intuitive.
198. I would already be psychic if I was meant to be.
199. It's not safe for me to follow my inner guidance.
200. I'm too stuck in analysis paralysis to be intuitive.

Journaling Pages for Statements 181 - 200

At times you have to leave the city of your comfort and go into the wilderness of your intuition. What you'll discover will be wonderful. What you'll discover is yourself.

Alan Alda

1. From the tapping statements between 1 – 20, list the top seven statements that you thought or felt applied to you:

1.

2.

3.

4.

5.

6.

7.

2. From this list of seven statements, select one and describe how it plays out in your life. Give an example or two. It is important to recognize and identify the pattern. Is there a trigger? How does it begin? How has it benefited you? How has it harmed you? For instance, did your intuition not answer the question you asked? Are you sure? Or did you not receive the answer you wanted to hear so you believed your question went unanswered?

3. Tap out the top 7 statements.

4. As you were tapping out the statements, did you have any flashback or memories of the past, any additional insights, and/or ah-ha thoughts? If so, write them down. Make note of them.

201 – 220 EFT Tapping Statements

Intuition does not come to an unprepared mind.

Albert Einstein

201. I don't know the right questions to ask my intuition.
202. I can't let go enough to trust the quiet voice within.
203. Logic and rationality are the sole guides for my life.
204. Intuition only comes through while in a trance state.
205. Intuition is synonymous with punishment and death.
206. The subtle intuitive messages are too subtle for me.
207. I'm a psychic sponge picking up everyone's feelings.
208. There is no place for intuition in my professional life.
209. My doubts interfere too much for me to be intuitive.
210. I am skeptical of the information I receive intuitively.
211. Being intuitive means my responses have to be right.
212. I don't know how to allow my intuition to just happen.
213. I don't know how to incorporate intuition into my life.
214. I will believe intuition is real when it has been proven.
215. My rational mind is in dispute with my inner guidance.
216. I ignore anything that cannot be logically understood.
217. I don't know how to incorporate guidance into my life.
218. Inner guidance is not synonymous with love and truth.
219. I'm not committed to experimenting with my intuition.
220. Others will think I am weird if I tell them I am intuitive.

© Tessa Cason, 2022.

Journaling Pages for Statements 201 – 220

Insight is not a light bulb that goes off inside our heads.
It is a flickering candle that can easily be snuffed out.

Malcolm Gladwell

1. From the tapping statements between 1 – 20, list the top seven statements that you thought or felt applied to you:

1.

2.

3.

4.

5.

6.

7.

2. From this list of seven statements, select one and describe how it plays out in your life. Give an example or two. It is important to recognize and identify the pattern. Is there a trigger? How does it begin? How has it benefited you? How has it harmed you? For instance, do you know how to word questions for your intuition? When learning a new skill, do you assume that you are supposed to know everything without study?

3. Tap out the top 7 statements.

4. As you were tapping out the statements, did you have any flashback or memories of the past, any additional insights, and/or ah-ha thoughts? If so, write them down. Make note of them.

© Tessa Cason, 2022.

221 – 240 EFT Tapping Statements

Intuition is knowing without knowing.

Anonymous

221. Intuitive insights are a product of creative imagination.
222. I'm not capable of receiving answers from my intuition.
223. Psychics are fat, toothless, and stare into a crystal ball.
224. I must know how it works before I can use my intuition.
225. I don't know how to word questions to ask my intuition.
226. It freaks me out that I know what they are going to say.
227. I must rely on the leader of the tribe for all my answers.
228. I don't know how to communicate with my spirit guides.
229. Others will think me weird if I do anything intuitive-like.
230. I don't understand what my intuition is trying to tell me.
231. Feeling powerless gets in the way of my being intuitive.
232. It would be too embarrassing to explore being intuitive.
233. I'm not capable of hearing the answers to my questions.
234. I don't know how to hold onto or remember my dreams.
235. I don't make time to learn the language of the Universe.
236. I must know how it works before I can trust my intuition.
237. I don't know how to determine if my intuition is accurate.
238. I don't understand the images, symbols, or pictures I see.
239. I am overwhelmed with the emotions of everyone I meet.
240. I don't have the ability to get useful information instantly.

© Tessa Cason, 2022.

Journaling Pages for Statements 221 – 240

*Practice listening to your intuition, your inner voice;
ask questions; be curious; see what you see; hear what
you hear; and then act upon what you know to be true.
These intuitive powers were given to your soul at birth."*

Clarissa Pinkola Estés

1. From the tapping statements between 1 – 20, list the top seven statements that you thought or felt applied to you:

1.

2.

3.

4.

5.

6.

7.

2. From this list of seven statements, select one and describe how it plays out in your life. Give an example or two. It is important to recognize and identify the pattern. Is there a trigger? How does it begin? How has it benefited you? How has it harmed you? For instance, do you have to know how intuition works before using it? Do you know how a car or computer or calculator works?

3. Tap out the top 7 statements.

4. As you were tapping out the statements, did you have any flashback or memories of the past, any additional insights, and/or ah-ha thoughts? If so, write them down. Make note of them.

241 – 260 EFT Tapping Statements

Don't try to comprehend with your mind.
Your minds are very limited. Use your intuition.

Madeleine L'Engle

241. I know I will not be able to translate the intuitive information.
242. I can't distinguish between my feeling, thoughts, and intuition.
243. I don't understand the metaphors and symbols of my intuition.
244. I can't detach enough to receive the answer from my intuition.
245. I don't know the difference between my mind and my intuition.
246. It isn't possible to know for sure what will happen in the future.
247. Intuition cannot provide precise, reliable, or useful information.
248. I don't know how to distinguish my thoughts from intuitive info.
249. Listening to my intuition cannot help me make better decisions.
250. To be intuitive means I must have the right answer immediately.
251. I don't know how to distinguish my intuition from other feelings.
252. I would be rejecting my religion if I develop my psychic abilities.
253. It isn't safe for me to advise others based on my inner guidance.
254. Wise and compassionate guidance is not always available to me.
255. I don't know how to translate metaphors into useful information.
256. It isn't okay for me to advise others based on my inner guidance.
257. I must understand what I am doing before I develop my intuition.
258. My conscious mind interferes with intuitive information I receive.
259. I don't know how to distinguish my intuition from other thoughts.
260. Intuitive insights are unpredictable and cannot be counted upon.

© Tessa Cason, 2022.

Journaling Pages for Statements 241 – 260

In order to trust your vibes, you have to first be able to sense them. To do this, you must quiet your mind.

Sonia Choquette

1. From the tapping statements between 1 – 20, list the top seven statements that you thought or felt applied to you:

1.

2.

3.

4.

5.

6.

7.

2. From this list of seven statements, select one and describe how it plays out in your life. Give an example or two. It is important to recognize and identify the pattern. Is there a trigger? How does it begin? How has it benefited you? How has it harmed you? For instance, can you distinguish between your feelings, thoughts, and intuition? Intuition is a skill. To be proficient at any skill, practice is required. Have you practiced?

3. Tap out the top 7 statements.

4. As you were tapping out the statements, did you have any flashback or memories of the past, any additional insights, and/or ah-ha thoughts? If so, write them down. Make note of them.

261 – 280 EFT Tapping Statements

*You will never follow your own inner voice
until you clear up the doubts in your mind.*

Roy T. Bennett

261. I don't understand the impressions my body experiences.
262. I am not in present time enough to have intuitive insights.
263. I am too frightening to share my intuitive hits with others.
264. It isn't safe for others to follow my inner guidance advice.
265. I don't know how to interpret and assemble intuitive data.
266. I would feel foolish if my intuition led me into a dark alley.
267. Listening to my intuition is synonymous with numbing out.
268. Others will think me crazy if I share my insights with them.
269. I don't know what it is supposed to feel like to be intuitive.
270. I don't connect my physical signals with intuitive feedback.
271. I don't know how to interpret the messages of my intuition.
272. I don't know how to integrate intuitive data with other data.
273. Intuitive information comes through in complete sentences.
274. I don't know how to interpret intuitive information I receive.
275. I override my intuition with logic, emotions, and/or intellect.
276. Intuition is not about receiving and interpreting information.
277. It isn't possible to accurately know something without proof.
278. I can't tell the difference between my mind and my intuition.
279. I don't know the questions to ask to clarify the info I receive.
280. I don't know how to discern if an answer is from my intuition.

Journaling Pages for Statements 261 – 280

Listen to the wind, it talks.
Listen to the silence, it speaks.
Listen to your heart, it knows.

Native American Proverb

1. From the tapping statements between 1 – 20, list the top seven statements that you thought or felt applied to you:

1.

2.

3.

4.

5.

6.

7.

2. From this list of seven statements, select one and describe how it plays out in your life. Give an example or two. It is important to recognize and identify the pattern. Is there a trigger? How does it begin? How has it benefited you? How has it harmed you? For instance, being intuitive requires that you are in present time. If you are in the future, you are surrounded by your fears. If you are in the past, you are dragging your anger around with you. How can you discern between intuition, anger, and fear?

3. Tap out the top 7 statements.

4. As you were tapping out the statements, did you have any flashback or memories of the past, any additional insights, and/or ah-ha thoughts? If so, write them down. Make note of them.

281 – 300 EFT Tapping Statements

There are a lot of voices inside of us. We have the voices of our parents, our grandparents, our society, our bosses, our own should's and shouldn'ts, and our self-worth is in us, controlling us a lot. When we can get past all of those, and get to the deep, core part of us, there's a voice within our soul that I believe is connected to our Divine or Higher Self. That voice within is there to guide us through all aspects of our lives.

Echo Bodine

281. I'm not willing to go step by step to learn how to use my intuition.
282. I'm uncomfortable receiving and articulating intuitive impressions.
283. Reading someone's mind is nothing more than reading body cues.
274. My fear of what others will think gets in the way of being intuitive.
285. I don't know the difference between intuition and wishful thinking.
286. I cannot understand what inner guidance wants me to understand.
287. I am supposed to totally understand the intuitive impressions I get.
288. Intuition is nothing but make-believe, pretend, or making things up.
289. I don't know how to formulate precise questions to ask my intuition.
290. I don't trust that the direction my intuition is leading me is the best.
291. If I was intuitive, it would tell me to do something I don't want to do.
292. I don't know the difference between self-talk info from intuitive info.
293. It isn't okay to share information I receive about someone with them.
294. Insights, intuition, and/or inspirations are not messages from my soul.
295. I don't know how to discern between correct message and false ones.
296. I don't know how to discern from whom the messages are coming from.
297. I know I will not be able to accurately translate the intuitive information.
298. I don't know how to distinguish my feelings from other people's feelings.
299. It's too confusing to tell whether I am following my inner guidance or not.
300. It freaks me out when I get feelings about someone just by touching them.

© Tessa Cason, 2022.

Journaling Pages for Statements 281 - 300

Intuition comes in several forms:

* a sudden flash of insight, visual or auditory
* a predictive dream
* a sense of knowing something already
* a sense of deja vu
* a snapshot image of a future scene or event
* a spinal shiver of recognition as something is occurring or told to you
* knowledge, perspective or understanding divined from tools which respond to the subconscious mind.

Sylvia Clare

1. From the tapping statements between 1 - 20, list the top seven statements that you thought or felt applied to you:

1.

2.

3.

4.

5.

6.

7.

2. From this list of seven statements, select one and describe how it plays out in your life. Give an example or two. It is important to recognize and identify the pattern. Is there a trigger? How does it begin? How has it benefited you? How has it harmed you? For instance, do you lack confidence in yourself to know if your intuition is taking you in the direction you want? Do you know where you want to go? Or is it easier to sit back and let life happen to you.

3. Tap out the top 7 statements.

4. As you were tapping out the statements, did you have any flashback or memories of the past, any additional insights, and/or ah-ha thoughts? If so, write them down. Make note of them.

© Tessa Cason, 2022.

Appendix

General Symbolism

Acorn: Potential, power, perseverance, hard work, strength, future potential.

Anchor: Security, support, steadiness, lack of movement, limitation, held back.

Armor/shield: Defense, protection, preparation, strength, guarded.

Bed: Need for rest and relaxation, healing.

Blindfold: Inability to see things clearly, to face the Truth and accept facts, to be honest with self. Focus on the inner world.

Caduceus: Health.

Chains: Restriction, bondage, conflict, lack of freedom, addictions.

Children: Promise, hope, fresh starts, new ideas, new beginnings, a fresh way at looking at the world, innocence.

Coins: Physical world, money, responsibility, generosity, dedication, grounded, health, determination.

Cups: Emotions, "my cup runneth over," transformations, receptivity.

Darkness: Uncertainty, sneakiness, depression, mystery, secrets, without full knowledge.

Earthquake: Shake-up of life, loss of control, "on shaky ground."

Feather: Light, airy, fun, playfulness, something previously used but no longer needed.

Flag: Announcement, transformation, change, shift in consciousness.

Gold: Power, spiritual gifts.

Globes: Whole world "at my fingertips," ideas, totality, comprehension, grasping the "big picture."

Gavel: Authority, power, judgment.

Hammer: Getting a point across, force, getting the job done, action, hammer out the details, hard work.

Jewels: Treasures, success, reward.

Keys: Truth, answers, opportunity, adventure, discovery, freedom.

Lantern: Awareness, insight, perception, clarity, illumination, understanding, Truth, vigilance, exploration.

Lemniscate/infinity symbol: Motion, endless and eternal energy, infinity, everlasting, balance.

Mirror: Reflection.

Oar: Change direction in life, movement; without an oar – lost momentum, feeling powerless.

Parachute: Adventure, safety, escape (from uncomfortable situation).

Phoenix: Rise from the ashes, mystical rebirth, transformation, resurrection.

Quicksand: Feeling stuck, hopeless, helpless, powerless, a losing situation.

Ring: Commitment, something meaningful, accomplishment.

Ropes: Confinement, bound, restriction, tied up in knots, togetherness.

Scale: Balance, harmony, precision, equilibrium.

Shoes: Protection, grounded, direction, approach to life, support.

Sunglasses: Self-image, "shading" or protecting self, wanting to control perception, distancing self and feelings.

Swords: Activity, power, decisiveness, protection, cut away negativity, bravery.

Landscape Symbols

Beach: Fun, relaxation, play, warmth, vacation, constant change.

Blue sky: Possibility, hope, limitless potential, freedom.

Clouds: Realization, ideas, thoughts, joy, revelation; fluffy cloud – contentment, uplifting; dark clouds – depression.

Desert: Emotionless, lacking in life force.

Fire: Passion, awareness, energy, ambition, power, inspiration, transformation, enlightenment, warmth, enthusiasm, spontaneity.

Fields: Fertile ground, new opportunities, new beginnings, hard work, "As we sow, so shall we reap."

Flowers: Beauty, joy, friendship, growth, caring, unfolding, opening up and receiving, kindness, fertility.

Forest: The unknown, lost perspective, feeling lost, "can't see the forest for the trees," infinity, wilderness.

Fruit: Fertility, harvest.

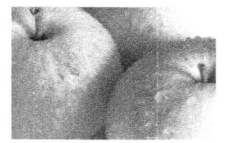

Gate: Open gate - new opportunities; closed gate – decisions need to be made.

Hills: Minor challenges, journey, awareness.

Ice: Isolation, separation, unexpressed emotions, contemplation of growth.

Leaves: Growth, vitality, new starts and beginnings, and/or a new chance in life…"Turning over a new leaf."

Light: Aliveness, spiritual illumination; lacking light – need to discover and/or inquire.

Lightning: Let go of old ideas, divine intervention, stuck in consciousness, flash of insight, upcoming storm.

Moon: Reflection, cycles, subconscious, intuition, emotions, imagination, feelings, femininity.

Mountains: Challenges, timelessness, attainment, strength, transitions, wisdom, understanding, barriers to overcome, success.

Ocean: Emotional depth, infinite possibilities, mystery.

Path/Pathway: Journey, distance to complete a goal, spiritual evolution, self-discovery.

Rain: Washing away the old, detoxification, nurturing, grief.

Rainbow: "Peace after the storm," God's grace, and blessings.

Rivers: Emotional flux, progress, movement of consciousness; still waters, stagnation.

Roads: Spiritual journey, choice, consciousness.

Rocks: Rocks have been around since creation, history, longevity, stability, grounding, healing.

Sea: The unconscious, emotions, mystery, dreams, power, travel.

Snow: "Out in the cold," isolation, difficulties, harsh conditions, quiet, beauty, clean, hibernation.

Star: Illumination, spirit, direction, guidance, Truth, navigation, compassion, hopes, life force, peace, Angelic presence, ideals.

Stones: Minor challenges. annoyances, obstacles in the way.

Stream: Flow of emotions, ideas and/or information, spiritual refreshment.

Sun: Warmth, nurturing, realization, illumination, courageous, endless, joy, wholeness; rising – new beginnings; setting-endings.

Trees: Strength, wisdom, sheltering, nobility, regeneration, healing.

Water: Emotions, love, Truth, knowledge, healing, depth, subconscious; calm – peace, serenity; rough – emotional trauma.

Wheat: Abundance, harvest, wisdom, fertility, sustenance.

Structure Symbolism

Airport: Beginning or ending of a process or journey, a desire to get away, take a break, or escape from something.

Alley: An indirect, secret, or out of the way route to get from one place to another; dark – danger.

Arch: Stability, support, gateways, transitions. New beginnings, direction, opportunities.

Bench: Taking time to re-evaluate, re-examine, rethink, taking a break, resting.

Brick Wall: Obstacles, stuck, paralysis, in need of solutions.

Bridge: Transitions to a new beginning, escaping difficulties, bridging the past and future, resources to move about difficulties.

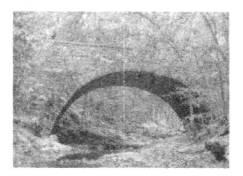

City/Village/Town: Gatherings of people, ideas, thoughts, energy, group effort to fulfill a common goal, protection.

Closet: A desire to clean out, re-organize, define, re-prioritize our lives and/or aspects of our lives.

Door: Passage, desire to open up, exploration, transition; stuck – feeling powerless; locked – being denied.

Escalator: Assistance, desiring something more, movement between levels of consciousness.

Fountain: Spiritual strength, nourishment, harmony, abundance, peace.

Hospital: Feeling under the weather and/or vulnerable, in need of healing, assistance to recover, and rest.

House: One's concept of self, safety, protection, stability, needs repair – a need to examine that which is not working.

Island: Separation, isolation, independence; deserted-wanting freedom from responsibilities; ; lush – abundance.

Ladder: Achievement, process and progress of fulfilling goals, different levers of consciousness.

© Tessa Cason, 2022.

Library: Knowledge, discovery, wisdom, entertainment.

Microscope: Study, observation, need to examine closely for clarity and understanding.

Prison: Lack or loss of freedom, punishment, discipline, infraction, restrictions.

Roof: Protection, an insightful perception, limitation.

Room: Activities, different aspects of our personality; kitchen-nurturing; living room-social interaction; bedroom-rest, relaxation.

Ruins: Feeling ruined and defeated, need to begin building a new life, letting go of the past, looking for treasures from the past.

Shelf: Being "shelved," stored, set aside, aspects of our lives (hobbies, history, self-help, home improvement.)

Ship: A voyage, the soul's journey, pleasure; stormy sea - emotional turbulence; calm sea - emotional rewards.

Stairs: Going upstairs - progress, moving forward in life; going downstairs - backpedaling, confusion.

Telephone: Being heard, communication, expressing one's self; ringing phone - subconscious wanting our attention.

Train: Absolute power, unstoppable, journey, direction, movement, momentum, massiveness.

Tunnel: Unknown, caution, one step at a time, subconscious mind.

Vehicles: Navigation, power, control, direction, innovation, image.

Wall: Separation, safety, compartmentalizing, privacy.

Wheel: Cycles of life, movement, Divine power, completion, travel, energy, creativity.

Windows: Introspection, observation from a distance, detachment, daydreaming.

Yacht: Luxury, success, abundance, travel, upper class.

Zoo: Imprisonment, confinement, separation from one's environment; life feels like a zoo, chaotic; exotic, foreign, or rare.

Basic Shapes Symbolism

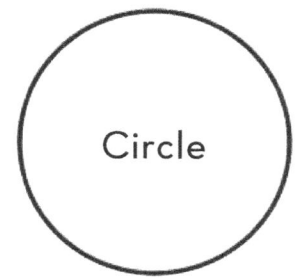

Keywords:

Life	Energy	Inclusion	Centering
Focus	Union	Wholeness	Life's Cycles
Unity	Infinite	Nurturing	Beginning
Motion	Cosmos	Initiation	Potential

Circle

Circles have no beginning or end. Their completeness suggests the infinite, unity, perfection, integrity, and wholeness. They are an archetypal form representing the sun, earth, moon, Universe, and other celestial objects.

Circles have free movement. They can roll. Their movement suggests energy and power. Circles protect, endure, and restrict. They confine what's within and keep things out. They offer safety as well as boundaries.

Circles are graceful and their curves are seen as feminine. They are comforting and give a sense of sensuality and love. Circles suggest community as well as warmth, tenderness, friendship, love, care, affection, and compassion.

Keywords:

Life	Unity	Balance	Explosive
Hope	Lively	Dynamic	Unification
Honor	Energy	Structure	Transition
Faith	Sacred	Temperance	Movement

Cross

Crosses symbolize spirituality and healing. They are seen as the meeting place of divine energies. The 4 points of a cross represent self, nature, wisdom, and higher power or being. Crosses suggest transition, balance, faith, unity, temperance, hope, and life.

They represent relationships, syntheses, and a need for connection to something, whether that something is a group, individual, self, or project-related.

Vertical shapes are seen as strong and horizontal shapes are seen as peaceful.

Sharp shapes are lively and youthful and are seen as more masculine.

© Tessa Cason, 2022.

Basic Shapes Symbolism

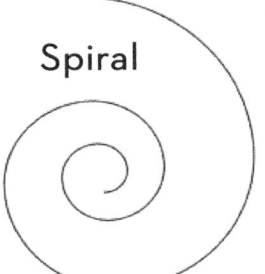

Spiral

Keywords:

Movement	Creativity	Release	Journey
Expansion	Progress	Centering	Evolution
Contraction	Growth	Direction	Letting go
Initiation	Release	Surrender	Life energy

Spirals are expressions of creativity. They are often found in the growth pattern of many organisms, suggesting growth and evolution. Spirals convey ideas of fertility, birth, death, expansion, and transformation. They are cycles of time, life, seasons, and are a common shape in religious and mystical symbolism.

Spirals move in either direction and represent returning to the same point on life's journey with new levels of understanding. They represent trust during change, the release of energy and maintaining flexibility through transformation.

Clockwise spirals represent projection of an intention and counterclockwise spirals the fulfillment of an intention.

Square

Keywords:

Power	Balance	Strength	Dependability
Truth	Integrity	Direction	Foundation
Structure	Pragmatic	Harmony	Proportion
Reliable	Ascension	Creativity	Permanence

Squares and rectangles are stable. They're familiar and trusted shapes that suggest honesty. They have right angles and represent order, mathematics, rationality, and formality. They are seen as earthbound.

Squares and rectangles suggest conformity, solidity, equality, dependability, security, and peacefulness.

They are four cardinal directions (north, south, east, west), four major season (winter, spring, summer, autumn), four cosmic elements (suns, moons, planets, stars), four prime elements (fire, earth, air, water), and four common phases of human life (birth, child, adult, death).

© Tessa Cason, 2022.

Basic Shapes Symbolism

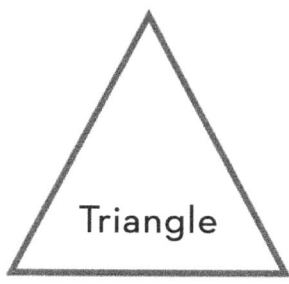

Keywords:

Triangle

Power	Strength	Portal	Manifestation
Harmony	Pragmatic	Ascension	Foundation
Integrity	Direction	Proportion	Integration
Reliable	Purpose	Doorway	Progression

Triangles can be stable when sitting on their base or unstable when not. They have energy and power. Their stability or lack of can suggest either conflict or strength. They represent action, dynamic tension, and aggression.

Triangles convey progression, direction, and purpose. They can direct movement based on which way they point.

The strength of triangles suggests masculinity. Triangles suggest self-discovery and revelation.

The triad is represented in the waxing, waning, and full moon; body, mind, and spirit; Father, Son, and Holy Ghost; mother, father, and child; past, present, and future.

Horizontal Lines

Keywords:

Tranquility
Feminine
Calm
Rest
Peaceful
Compose
Still

Vertical lines

Keywords:

Strength
Masculinity
Power
Aggression
Courage
Dominate

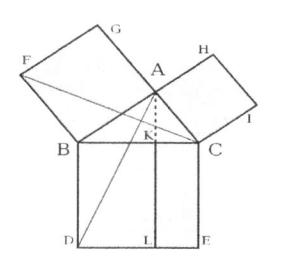

Sharp-angled Lines

Keywords:

Energy
Lively
Youthful
Explosive
Dynamic
Movement

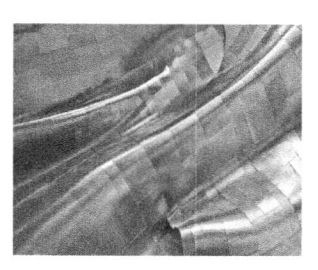

Soft Curves

Keywords:

Rhythm
Movement
Happiness
Pleasure
Generosity
Femininity

© Tessa Cason, 2022.

Color Significance

Blue
* Wisdom
* Truth
* Loyalty
* Tranquil
* Peaceful
* Sincere
* Comfort
* Ideas
* Trustworthy
* Conservatism
* Dependable
* Acceptance
* Inner Strength
* Fifth Chakra
* Verbal Communication

Black
* Power.
* Strength, force.
* Protective.
* Depth.
* Wealth.
* Sexuality.
* Fear.
* Death.
* Seriousness.
* Authority, prestige.
* Sophistication, elegance, classy.
* Formality, dignity.
* Sadness, grief, mourning.
* Stability, reliability.
* Emptiness, void.
* Unknown, mystery.
* Evil, darkness.

Brown
* Grounding.
* Earth.
* Fertility.
* Practical.
* Hard work.
* Reliable.
* Durable.
* Simplicity
* Longevity.
* Nurturing.
* Strength.
* Discernment.
* Contentment.
* Stability, solid.
* New beginnings.
* All things natural.

Gold
* Successful.
* Integrity.
* Respect.
* Dynamic.
* High quality.
* Wisdom.
* Happiness.
* Authentic.
* Inner knowledge.
* Money, wealth.
* Prestige, status.
* Triumphant.
* Absolute best.
* Golden Oldie.
* Golden rule.
* As good as gold.

Gray
* Neutral.
* Professional.
* Illness.
* Modesty.
* Maturity.
* Timeless.
* Dignified.
* Pessimistic.
* Frustration.
* Middle-of-the-road.
* Practical, reliable, durable.
* Intellect, knowledge, wisdom.
* Conservative.
* Authoritative.

Green
* Nature
* Renewal
* Healing
* Nurturing
* Hopeful
* Restful
* Wealth
* Success
* Fertility
* Harmony
* Freshness
* Compassionate
* Transformation
* Contemplative
* Fourth Chakra
* Heart Energy

Indigo
* Introspection.
* Thoughts.
* Knowledge.
* Integrity.
* Perception.
* Sympathetic.
* Visionary.
* Fearlessness.
* Idealistic.
* Fulfillment.
* Self-mastery.
* Insight intuition.
* Understanding.
* Sixth Chakra.
* Wisdom, knowledge, understanding.

© Tessa Cason, 2022.

Color Significance

Orange
* Social
* Optimistic
* Creative
* Imaginative
* Empathetic
* Friendly
* Resilience
* Sensuality
* Happy & Jovial
* Playful and Fun
* Zest & Vitality
* Flamboyancy
* Vibrancy
* Confidence
* Second chakra
* Emotions

Purple
* Spirituality
* Royalty
* Idealistic
* Wisdom
* Dignity
* Elegance
* Mysticism
* Awareness
* Inspirational
* Visionary
* Introspective
* Empathetic
* Knowledge
* Enlightenment
* Seventh chakra
* Higher Consciousness

Pink
* Loving.
* Kindness.
* Gentle.
* Patient.
* Joyful.
* Playful.
* Exciting.
* Happiness.
* Passionate.
* Affection.
* Sensitivity.
* Compassion.
* Sensuality.
* Lighthearted.
* Acceptance.
* Youthful.

Red
* Love
* Passion
* Energy
* Action
* Speed
* Courage
* Strength
* Vitality
* Danger
* Excitement
* Impulsive
* Confidence
* Determination
* Independence
* First chakra
* Grounded

Turquoise
* Healing.
* Refreshing.
* Friendly.
* Growth.
* Uplifting.
* Perception.
* Discerning.
* Idealistic.
* Contentment.
* Concentration.
* Compassionate.
* Communication.
* Calming, soothing.
* Tranquility, serenity.
* Clarity of thought.
* Empathetic, caring.

White
* Consciousness.
* Awareness.
* Truth.
* Wisdom.
* Inspiration.
* Divine.
* Precision.
* Fairness.
* Simplicity.
* Goodness.
* Peace, calm.
* Cleanliness.
* Innovations.
* Compassionate.
* Fresh beginnings.
* Purity, innocence.

Yellow
* Optimism
* Inner Joy
* Caution
* Warmth
* Sunshine
* Happiness
* Brightness
* Analytical
* Creativity
* Curiosity
* Self-respect
* Mental Activities
* Contentment
* Focus, deduction
* Third Chakra
* Personal Power

© Tessa Cason, 2022.

Number Keywords

1

New beginnings
Initiator of action
Pioneers
Inventive ideas
Independent
Individualistic
Determination
Creative
Original
Assertive
Willful
Progressive
Strong willed

2

Balance
Tactful
Duality
Partnerships
Communication
Cooperation
Adaptability
Desire for harmony
Diplomatic
Peaceful
Adaptable
Understanding
Receptive
Gentleness

3

Imaginative
Creative
Artistic
Versatility
Self-expressive
Verbalization
Inspiration
Adventurous
Communicative
Optimistic & positive
Sociable & friendly
Outgoing
Happy & fun-loving
Joy of living

4

Foundation
Stability & Solidity
Conservative
Pragmatism
Hard-working
Organization & Order
Steady growth
Practical & Logical
Trustworthy & Helpful
Self-disciplined
Service
Loyal
Home
Attention to detail

5

Freedom
Change
Unpredictability
Instability
Motion
Adventure
Resourceful
Expansion
Flexible
Evolution
Versatile
Adaptable
Exploratory
Mental Curiosity

6

Responsibility
Service & Idealism
Truth & Integrity
Trustworthy
Compassionate
Community
Nurturing
Protection & Sincere
Balance & Stability
Honesty
Logical
Understanding
Conservation
Constructive

© Tessa Cason, 2022.

Number Keywords

7
Spirituality
Knowledge
Reclusive
Introspective & quiet
Peace & solitude
Understanding
Awareness & wisdom
Intuitive & perceptive
Philosophical
Inspirational
Esoteric
Mental analysis
Scientific research
Truthful
Observant

8
Personal power
Business
Success
Wealth
Executive abilities
Sound judgment
Ambitious
Decisive & commanding
Authoritative
Accomplished
Materialism
Leadership
Self-reliance
Determination

9
Fulfillment
Attainment
Satisfaction
Accomplishment
Humanitarian
Sympathetic
Helpful
Completion & Endings
Compassion
Generosity
Benevolence
Patience
Charity
Philanthropy

11
Fulfillment
Vision
Idealistic
Intuitive
Giver
Innovator
Mass communication
Idealist & Dreamer
Inspirational
Revelation
Spiritual
Teacher
Achievement
Individualist

22
Master builder
Idealist
Visionaries
Achiever
Wisdom
Intense
Idealistic
Resourceful
Passionate.
Manifestation
Awareness
Industrious
Insightful
Optimistic

0
Blessings
Potential
Possibility
Void
Totality
Rebirth
Limitless
Truth
Purity
All That Is
Consciousness
Freedom
All & Nothing
Yin & Yang

© Tessa Cason, 2022.

Chakras

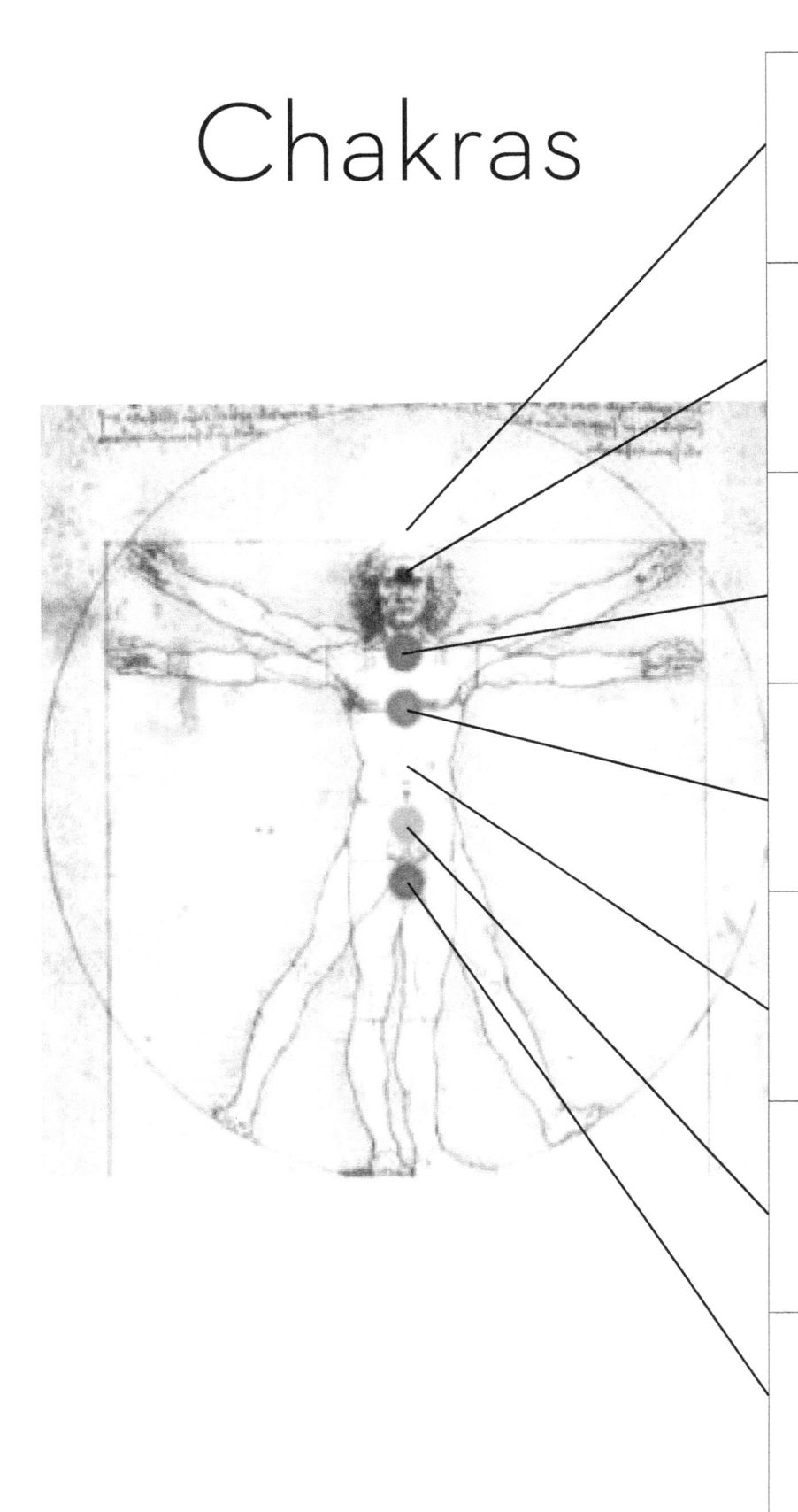

7th – Crown Chakra
Top of the Head
Higher/Ideal/Spiritual Self
Element – Light
Physical Colors – Purple, White, Gold, Silver

6th – Brow Chakra
Between the Eyebrows
Insight Intuition, The Mind, and Our Belief Systems
Element – Space
Physical Color – Indigo

5th – Throat Chakra
Throat
Self-Expression, Communication, and Discernment Abilities
Element – Ether
Physical Color – Sky Blue

4th – Heart Chakra
Heart
All Forms of Love and Relationships, Compassion
Element – Air
Physical Color – Green

3rd – Solar Plexus Chakra
Navel to Diaphragm
Personal Power, Actions We Take in the Physical World
Element – Fire
Physical Color – Yellow

2nd – Sacral Chakra
Lower Abdomen to Navel
Emotional Tools for Creating, Sexuality, Hopes, Wishes
Element – Water
Physical Color – Orange

1st – Base Chakra
Base of the Spine
Survival, Security, Basic Needs, Tribe, Grounding, Wealth
Element – Earth
Physical Colors – Red, Black, Brown

Information provided does not substitute for professional medical advice and care.

© Tessa Cason, 2022.

Introduction

Traditionally, there are 7 major energy systems located within our etherical body called chakras. Chakra is a Sanskrit word meaning "wheel." "Energy" is our "vital force." Our etherical body is the "energy field" that surrounds the physical body.

An analogy of a chakra would be this:

There is a network of streets (passageways of energy). Where several streets cross is called an intersection (or chakra). Each chakra has its own significance, qualities, and lessons relating to our physical, mental, emotional, and spiritual selves.

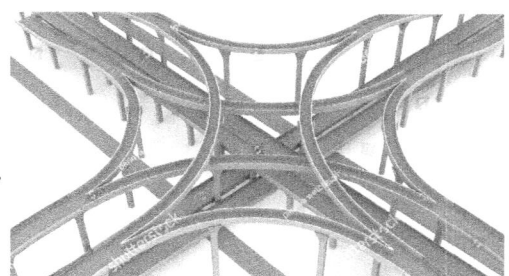

1st, 2nd, and 3rd Chakras: Represents the five-sensory, the physical and emotional selves that has the power and passion to take action...fueled by the thoughts, attitudes and beliefs of the other 4 chakras.

4th Chakra: Represents the integration of the multi-sensory self with the five sensory self, the spiritual, mental, emotional, and physical self.

5th, 6th, 7th, Chakras: Represents the multi-sensory self, the spiritual and mental selves, based on our beliefs, thoughts, attitudes, choices, and decisions.

© Tessa Cason, 2022.

Root or 1st Chakra

Tools, Skills, Abilities, Capabilities Necessary to Function in the Physical World
Survival, Security, Basic Needs, Tribe/Family
Physical Beingness, Grounding, Stability, Foundation, Financial Wealth

Location: Base of the spine.

Element: Earth

Keywords for the 1st Chakra:

Vitality	Courage	Confident	Survival	Grounding	Security
Aliveness	Home	Discipline	Stability	Physical Body	Vivacious
Competent	Skillful	Proficient	Moxie	Foundation	Talent
Adept	Bold	Energetic	Fearless	Wherewithal	Audacious
Self-assured	Aggressive	Safety	Family	Self-preservation	Energy

Qualities/Characteristics/Lessons:
* Physical beingness.
* Tools, skills, abilities, and capabilities necessary to function in the physical world including aliveness, confidence, courage, fearlessness, adventurous, energetic, audacious, aggressive, self-assured, vigorous, bold, vivaciousness.
* Links the individual with the physical world.
* Survival and basic life needs and necessities...including financial prosperity and money.
* Inner strength, vitality.
* Matters relating to the material world...safety, grounding, stability, security, courage.
* Mastery of self, fully alive, unlimited physical energy.
* Feeling grounded.
* Can stand up for self.
* Feels at home in the physical world.

Physical Color: Red, black, and brown

Spiritual Color: Red

Glands/Organs: Feet, ankles, knees, legs. Base of spine. Immune system. Bones and bone marrow. Rectum. Male reproductive organs. (A man's sexual organs are located primarily in his first chakra. Survival of the species has been the responsibility of the male. Thus male sexual energy is usually experienced primarily as physical, survival, and as a basic need.

Whereas, a woman's sexual organs are located primarily in her second chakra, the emotional chakra. A woman usually approaches sex through her emotions. Both the first and the second chakras are associated with sexual energy.)

Deficient Characteristics:
* Lacks courage, self-confidence to stand up for self.
* Cannot get feet on the ground, lacks grounding.
* Basic and survival needs not being met…including financial.
* Does not feel safe in the world and/or does not want to be in the physical body.
* Not in present time.
* Timid, apprehensive, cowardly, distressed, worthless, damaged goods, broken, unfixable.
* Martyr, victim. (Martyr – A person who creates drama in their life where there was none in an attempt to gain sympathy and pity from those around them.)
* Fearful of anything and everything.
* Needing to ground through physical weight.
* Has little interest in sex.
* Sluggish, lazy, tired.
* Fearful, anxious, restless, lack of discipline.
* Financial difficulties.

Excessive Energy:
* Clinging to security, hoarding possessions.
* Fear of change, rigid.
* Forced confidence when scared to death! Feels inadequate, helpless, powerless. Puts up a false facade of bravery and courageousness.
* Overly concerned with one's physical survival.
* Materialism, greed.
* Obesity, overeating.

Malfunctions: Obesity, anorexia, eating disorders, malnourished, hemorrhoids, lower back problems and pain, sciatica. Problems with feet, knees, legs including varicose veins. Sexual problems, sexual diseases. Adrenal insufficiency, lack of energy. Rectal or colon cancer. Skin problems. Depression. Immune-related disorders.

Spleen or 2nd Chakra

Emotional Tools for Creating and Being Creative
Aspirations, Desires, Hopes, Wishes, Yearnings
Sexuality, Sensuality, Lust

Location: Lower abdomen to navel

Element: Water

Keywords for the 2nd Chakra:

Aspirations	Emotions	Desires	Creativity	Intimacy	Yearnings
Sensuality	Sexuality	Imagination	Visioning	Expectations	Passion
Excitement	Enthusiasm	Devotion	Lust	Vitality	Fulfillment

Qualities/Characteristics/Lessons:
* Aspirations, desires, hopes, wishes, yearnings.
* Emotional tools for creating, for being creative…imagination, expectation, visioning, passion, inspiration, devotion, enthusiasm, excitement.
* Sexuality, sensuality, lust.
* Allow one's self to feel the joy of life, to feel the full range of emotions!
* Joyful, warm, humorous, laughter, friendly, upbeat, full of zest and vitality. Outgoing, relaxed, cheerful, expressive, spontaneous. Flexibility. Go with the flow.

Physical Color: Orange

Spiritual Color: Yellow

Glands/Organs: Ovaries, womb. Low back, hips/pelvis, buttocks. Colon, bladder, pancreas, small intestines, kidneys, lymphatic system, all the body fluids.

Deficient Characteristics:
* Won't allow desires and/or dreams nor expect them to be fulfilled.
* Closed emotionally. Feeling separate from. Lonely. Feeling unloved.
* Feeling impoverished emotionally.
* Feeling inadequate, helpless, and/or everything is hopeless.
* Not wanting to feel anything emotionally.
* Worries about needs being met.
* Would rather detach from self and/or others, their life, and from life.

© Tessa Cason, 2022.

* Difficulties connecting to one's own creativity.
* Fearful of being sexual, of being "vulnerable." Closed down sexually. Difficulty connecting to sexual self. Inhibited. Infrequent and dissatisfying sex.
* Tendency to avoid pleasure, lack of passion, lack of sexuality and sensuality.
* Unable to maintain long-term, fulfilling, significant-other, emotional, sexual relationships.
* Doesn't know how to take care of themselves and/or others.
* Feeling there isn't sweetness in their life.
* Unwilling to meet their own and/or their partner's emotional and/or sexual needs and desires. Clueless when it comes to emotional needs, theirs or anyone else's.
* Poor social skills.
* Fear of sex, lack of desire, passion, excitement, denial of pleasure.
* Fear of change.
* Rigidity in attitudes.

Excessive Energy:
* Doesn't expect their desires and/or dreams to be fulfilled. Doesn't believe nor trust that their needs will be provided for nor met.
* Overly emotional. Emotionally explosive, volatile, out of control. Emotional see-saw. Ruled by emotions…a swamp and/or a hurricane emotionally. Destructive emotionally.
* Fabricates emotions to feel alive. Will hurt self and/or create pain for the body so as to feel.
* Needs to exaggerate feelings so as to be able to feel anything.
* Over-eats. Loves to and indulges in the senses of tastes.
* Weight problems…to avoid intimacy and sexuality.
* Constant need for pleasurable stimulation, entertainment, partying, and/or social interactions.
* Sexual addiction, seductive manipulation.
* Obsessive attachment.
* Emotional dependency.

Malfunctions: Cancer of the colon, vagina, uterus. Bladder infections. Ovarian cysts and/or cancer, fibroids, endometriosis, pelvic inflammatory disease, menstrual dysfunction. Prostate problems and/or cancer. Emotional instability or numbness. Low sexual desire, impotence, frigidity, sexual problems, sexual dysfunction, promiscuity. Bowel problems, irritable bowel syndrome, ulcerative colitis, Crohn's disease, diverticulitis. Chronic low back pain and/or sciatica. Bladder and/or urinary problems.

Solar Plexus or 3rd Chakra

Actions We Take in the Physical World
Put the Foot to the Pedal and the Pedal to the Metal!
Personal Power, Perseverance
Gut Intuition

Location: Navel to diaphragm.

Element: Fire

Keywords for the 3rd Chakra:

Personal Power	Identify	Intuition	Energy	Control	Action
Accomplishment	Adversity	Authority	Trustworthy	Movement	Deeds
Independence	Achievement	Triumph	Perseverance	Realization	Goals
Joy of Life	Will	Attainment	Intelligence	Persistence	Doing

Qualities/Characteristics/Lessons:
* Takes action…puts the foot to the pedal and the pedal to the metal.
* In touch with, listens to and follows gut intuition.
* Lives in present time.
* Inner strength, independence, strength of character, and will.
* Power as it relates to the self…feelings of being worthy, valuable, likeable, and confident.
* Ability to transform themselves and their life.
* Understands that every challenge is an opportunity to learn…the game of life does not build character, but reveals it.
* Possesses the qualities of perseverance and endurance.
* Acts as if everything was up to them. Prays as if everything was up to God.

Physical Color: Yellow

Spiritual Color: Blue

Organs/Glands: Digestive organs: pancreas, stomach, liver, gall bladder, duodenum, upper intestines, pancreas, kidney, adrenals. Mid-back. The respiratory system, breath, and diaphragm. The sympathetic nervous system.

Deficient Characteristics:
* Not taking the necessary action in their life.
* Feeling disempowered.
* Control issues…fearful of losing control and/or being controlled.

© Tessa Cason, 2022.

* Fear of power, of being powerful. Not safe to be powerful. Not willing to be powerful. Powerless.
* Not in present time.
* Unable/unwilling to establish and maintain boundaries to protect self. Let's other walk all over them, abuse them.
* Fear and/or an unwillingness to be accountable and responsible.
* Not in touch nor willing to trust gut intuition.
* Has no sense of their identity. Lacks self-respect. Has no sense of self-worth.
* Fearful of just about everything and everyone including authority, confrontation.
* Lacks self-discipline to achieve goals, to stay focused.
* Plays victim, martyr, and saboteur. Victim mentality.
* Feels as if every challenge is a personal attack to destroy them. Helpless and hopeless.
* Lacks self-confidence. Dependent. Worried about what others will think.
* Stays in a confused state to avoid taking action.
* Unable and unwilling to make decisions for themselves.
* Gives up to soon, too easily. Ready to throw in the towel. Feels like a failure, damaged goods, a loser. Wants to give up every time anything goes wrong. No stamina or endurance.
* Lacks ambition.
* Not willing to claim ownership of their own life. Doesn't believe they co-create their life. Not willing to take responsibility for their life.
* Sensitive to criticism.
* Frequently feels overwhelmed.
* Refuses to take in the fullness of life. Would rather shut down. Fearful that someone will take away anything they create, produce, or is of value to them.
* Timid and/or takes a submissive approach to life.
* Feeling worthless. Has no value to self and/or others.
* Low energy, chronic fatigue, addicted to stimulating substances.
* Poor self-esteem.
* Passive, fearful.
* Victim mentality, blaming others.
* Unreliable.
* Anxiety about the future.
* Oversensitive to what other people say and/or think.
* Nervous.
* Indecisive.

Excessive Energy:
* Doesn't feel anything will happen unless they make it happen. Won't accept help from anyone including God.
* Judgmental. Always right.
* Overly aggressive, manipulative, domineering, dominating, controlling, blaming.
* Self-destructive. Sabotages their life as well as those around them.
* Wants to dominate everything and everyone.
* Acts like a tyrannical child.

* Wants others to always be off guard. They want the upper hand and will do whatever to acquire and maintain the advantage. Always on the offensive.
* Sets unattainable standards for self and others.
* Confrontational, combative, challenging, belligerent, competitive, always finding fault with others.
* Feels alone in the world, without support from family, friends, and/or God/Divine/Spirit.
* Forceful in everything they do. Will not allow anyone to make decisions for them.
* Rigid boundaries so as to distance themselves from others.
* Workaholic. They can do it better than anyone else.
* Doesn't trust inner guidance and/or believe there is such a thing. If there is such a thing, it is not to be trusted. Only the mind can be trusted.
* Will not change direction in their life even when it is obvious a different path should be taken. To change the path before accomplishing the goal is seen as failure.
* Addicted to rage. Doesn't know how to handle anger appropriately.
* Lacks self-worth. Acts superior to hide their inferiority complex.
* Arrogance, power-hungry, stubbornness.
* Excessively ambitious and competitive

Malfunctions: Liver, gall bladder, adrenal, stomach, duodenal, intestinal, kidney and/or heart problems including cancer, ulcers, hepatitis, pancreatitis, diabetes, gall stones, heart attacks, infections, adrenal exhaustion. Intestinal, digestive and/or metabolic problems including hypoglycemia, diverticulitis, acid reflux, and/or constipation. Eating disorders such as anorexia, bulimia, or obesity. Addictions (issues of fear and control) to substances that give the illusion of energy, such as caffeine, sugar, amphetamines, or cocaine. Excessive weight around the middle. Sunken diaphragm. Inability to get a deep breath through the belly. Arthritis. Chronic Fatigue Syndrome.

Heart or 4th Chakra

Connection to God/Spirit/Universe/Divine
All Forms of Love: Divine Love, Romantic Love, Conditional Love,
Unconditional Love, Self Love, Self-esteem (Earned Love)
All Forms of Relationships: With the Self,
With Others Including Friends, Family/Tribe, Romantic Partner
Forgiveness, Compassion, Acceptance
The Soul is the Student and Teacher

Location: Region of the heart.

Element: Air

Keywords for the 4th Chakra:

Compassion	Harmony	Forgiveness	Love	Relationship	Balance
Unconditional Love	Breath	Acceptance	Grace	Openness	Ecstasy
Abandonment	Growth	Tranquility	Truth	Dedication	Respectful
Transformation	Serenity	Empathy	Peace	Loving	Reverence
Receiving and Giving	Nirvana	Service	Bliss	Hope	Kindness
Unity with All of Life	Bravery	Fulfillment	Joy	Integration	Empathy

Qualities/Characteristics/Lessons:
* Connection to Divine/God/Goddess/Universe/Spirit.
* All forms of love: Divine love, romantic love, unconditional and conditional love, self-love, self-esteem (earned love).
* All forms of relationships: With the self, with others including friends, family/tribe, romantic partner as well as everything in the Universe.
* Integration of spiritual self with physical self.
* Forgiveness, compassion, understanding, empathy as well as hatred, bitterness, grief, anger, jealousy.
* Transformation of the self through love, awareness, and forgiveness.
* The breath...taking in life.
* Harmony, tranquility, serenity, peace.
* Heaven, nirvana...on earth, in the physical body!
* The exchange of love...giving and receiving, loving and being loved.
* Grace...blessings from above.

Physical Color: Green (secondary color is pink)

© Tessa Cason, 2022.

Spiritual Color: White, gold

Organs/Glands: Heart, circulatory system, blood. Shoulders, arms, hands. Lungs, bronchial. Upper back, rib cage, chest.

Deficient Characteristics:
* Heart is closed down. Overly detached from the world.
* Emotional pain.
* Refuses to forgive self and/or anyone else. Forgiveness is seen as weakness.
* Angry at and/or punishing God and/or self.
* Doesn't believe in God's grace and/or there is a Higher Power.
* Feeling abandoned by God/Divine/Spirit/Universe.
* Unable to accept and/or give love to others as well as to self. Will not nurture or nourish self and/or others. Fearful of intimacy and relationships.
* Fearful of merging with Spirit and/or of losing self.
* Fearful of merging with another and/or of losing one's own identity.
* Fearful of being abandoned, rejected, of not being enough, of not being good enough.
* Not deserving and/or feeling unworthy of love. Feeling unlovable.
* Fearful of being free and/or feeling blissful.
* Fearful of loving, of being hurt, of being vulnerable, of letting go, of being abandoned by others and/or God.
* Unable and/or unwilling to take in the breath of life.
* Unable and/or unwilling to give of the self, to give and/or receive love. Fearful of any sort of relationships.
* Issues relating to commitment, forgiveness, bitterness, intimacy, jealousy, rejection, and/or resentment.
* Everything is either sensual and sexual or rational, logical, and intellectual because the inner feeling is missing.
* Lack of depth and warmth. No compassion or empathy for self and/or for others.
* Distrustful of others particularly their kindness. Suspects a reason or motive other than kindness.
* Uncomfortable when things are going well or are peaceful. "Waiting for the other shoe to drop."
* Holding onto past pain(s) involving a friendship and/or a significant-other, romantic, sexual relationship and/or a situation near and dear to the heart including "loss" of a marriage, an individual, job, etc.
* Feeling as if they are damaged goods, undesirable, scum of the earth, broken.
* Feeling lonely, isolated, and withdraw. Fearful of interpersonal relationships.
* Demanding and/or overly critical.
* Antisocial, withdrawn, cold, shy.
* Lacks tolerance for self and/or others.
* Is critical, judgmental, depressed, bitter, and lacks empathy.

Excessive Energy:
* Sadness.
* Moody, melodramatic, manic-depressive.
* Gullible and/or naive unless has a strong 3rd and 5th charka.
* Lonely.
* Leads with their heart.
* Doesn't always think things through.
* Overly sensitive to other people's pain.
* Strong desire to "fix" everything for others as well as for themselves.
* Grieves over the world's harsh and painful conditions.
* Depressed, rude, resentful.
* Demanding, jealousy, and/or possessive.
* Co-dependency.

Malfunctions: Breathing problems including asthma, bronchitis and/or pneumonia. Spleen and/or kidney problems. Heart and/or circulatory problems, angina, heart attacks, high blood pressure, asthma, allergies, congestive heart failure, chest pain, arteriosclerosis, shortness of breath. Breast cancer, tumors, lumps.

Throat or 5th Chakra

Self-expression, Communication
Decisions and Choices of How We Live Our Lives
Destiny Meets Free Will
Discernment Abilities
Courage to Live Our Inner Truth

Location: Area of the throat.

Element: Ether.

Keywords for the 5th Chakra:

Communication	Discernment	Perception	Insightful	Awareness	Wisdom
Self-Expression	Knowledge	Integrity	Understanding	Judgment	Sadness
Strength of Will	Determination	Astuteness	Consciousness	Courage	Choices

Qualities/Characteristics/Lessons:
* Self-expression, communication.
* Choices and decisions based on beliefs and attitudes.
* Strength of will and integrity (honesty with one's self).
* Decisive and able to make decisions.
* Trust discernment abilities.
* Courage to live one's life in truth.
* Sadness, when we get a lump in our throat.
* Courage. Takes on challenges.
* Responsible and accountable for own truth.

Physical Color: Blue.

Spiritual Color: Light blue.

Organs/Glands: Neck, throat, vocal cords, voice, trachea, larynx, esophagus. Mouth, jaw, teeth, gums. Thyroid, parathyroid, hypothalamus.

Deficient Characteristics:
* Poor verbal skills, shyness, cannot express thoughts.
* Suffocating, unable to breathe freely.

© Tessa Cason, 2022.

* Difficulties in speaking one's mind, expressing emotions. Fear of speaking up. Inability to express oneself clearly.
* Difficulties with making decisions for one's self...child, victim, and/or saboteur is in charge of making decisions.
* Difficulty making decisions if given too many choices. Cannot discern which choice would be for their highest and best good.
* Lack of discernment skills...doesn't trust self.
* Lacks the will to live. Life is hopeless. Would rather be dead than alive.

Excessive Energy:
* Arrogant. No one knows as much as them.
* Self-righteous.
* Talks too much with very little substance.
* Inability to listen.
* Loves to gossip.
* Interrupts others when someone else is talking.
* Stutters.
* Needs to be in control. Will never surrender control to anyone...for any reason.

Malfunctions: Sore throats. Speech problems including laryngitis, a voice without resonance. Raspy throat, chronic sore throat, mouth ulcers, laryngitis, swollen glands. Ear infections and problems. Stiff and/or knotted shoulders and neck, tension in the neck. TMJ. Difficulties with teeth and gums. Thyroid problems. Backaches and headaches. Tension in the eyes.

Brow or 6th Chakra

Insight Intuition
The Mind...Conscious, Subconscious
Belief System/Structural Framework/Blueprint
Thoughts and Attitudes
Mind Chatter - Our Teacher

Location: Between the eyebrows.

Element: Space

Keywords for the 6th Chakra:

Intelligence	Beliefs	Thoughts	Clairvoyance	Attitudes
Conscious & Subconscious Mind	Knowledge	Demeanor	Imagination	Ideology
Insight Intuition	Vision	Reasoning	Conceptual	Perception

Qualities/Characteristics/Lessons:
* Insight intuition.
* The mind...conscious, subconscious.
* The eye of wisdom that looks from within and sees truth. The wisdom of the mind gives direction to the compassion of the heart, just as compassion gives warmth and love to the clarity of insight.
* Search for truth...Truth vs. Illusion. Peace of mind.
* Our belief system, the structural framework for how we live our lives.
* Our thoughts and attitudes as a result of the beliefs.
* Intelligent, strong intellectual and deductive abilities, able to assimilate information.

Physical Color: Indigo

Spiritual Color: Blue

Organs/Glands: Pituitary and pineal glands. Face, eyes, ears, nose, sinus, face. Cerebellum. Central nervous system.

Deficient Characteristics:
* Rigid, fixed, or closed thinking.
* Inability to learn or comprehend, learning disabilities.

* Resistance to new and/or different ideas.
* Unwillingness to learn or comprehend.
* Lacks focus. Undisciplined and/or scattered thoughts.
* Mental stagnation.
* Lacks imagination.
* Difficulty visualizing, difficulty seeing the future.

Excessive Energy:
* Depression.
* Feeling disconnected from other people.
* Identifying with our "story," the drama of our life.
* Believing the illusion.
* Arrogant, prideful, not open to the ideas of others.
* Manipulative.
* Authoritarian.
* Up in the head and/or obsessive thinking.
* Not willing to learn our "lessons."
* Hallucination, nightmares, obsessions, and/or delusions.
* Difficulty concentrating,

Malfunctions: Headaches. Ear, eye, nose, and/or sinus problems. Blindness. Extreme sensitivity to lights, sounds, and/or other environmental factors. Nervous behaviors, paranoia, and/or any distortion of reality. Neurological disturbances including Multiple Sclerosis, polio, Parkinson's disease, seizures. Brain tumors. Strokes. Learning disabilities. Nightmares, hallucinations.

Crown or 7th Chakra

Higher/Ideal/Spiritual Self
Transcendent Intuition/All Knowing
Mystical Connection
Surrender
Biological Cell Memory
Past Life Data Bank/Memory
Spiritual Beingness (Spirit Resides in Each Cell of the Physical Body)

Location: Top of the head.

Element: Light

Keywords for the 7th Chakra:

Expanded Consciousness	Devotion	Celebration	Spirit	Divinity	Integration
Universal Consciousness	Selflessness	Purity	Values	Altruistic	Spirituality
All Knowingness	Serenity	Mysticism	Ethics	Reverence	Visionary
Humanitarianism	Worship	Beingness	Wisdom	Wholeness	Memories
Spiritual Awakening	Awareness	Karma	Grace	Purpose	Surrender

Qualities/Characteristics/Lessons:
* Spiritual/ideal/higher self.
* On purpose, on track with life mission, goals, dreams, visions and sacred contracts.
* Following one's dreams.
* Selflessness, altruistic, spirituality, devotional.
* Able to see the big picture.
* Connected to Divine wisdom.
* Allowing and accepting of mysticism into our life.
* Selfless service...without an agenda and/or attachment to the outcome.
* Surrender and transcendence of the individual self to the Divine self...moving away from the small, limited, physical self to merge and embrace a deeper, broader, spiritual self.
* Divine wisdom and understanding.
* Stores memories.

Physical Color: Violet, white, gold, silver.

Spiritual Color: White.

Organs/Glands: Cerebrum. Muscular and skeletal systems. Skin.

Deficient characteristics:
* Alienation, depression.
* Confusion, boredom, apathy.
* No spark of joy, catatonic.
* Fear of inner self, anything introspective, and/or spiritual.
* Totally unaware and chooses to remain unaware.
* Lack of inspiration.
* Closed to all spirituality and/or spiritually stagnated.
* Not willing to be accountable and responsible for their own life.
* Lack of self-awareness and/or sense of higher consciousness.
* Has no purpose and/or lacks a willingness to be on purpose with life.
* Apathetic.
* Materialistic.
* Dissociation between physical body and spiritual being.

Excessive Energy:
* Needing to be perfect, makes lots of judgments, particularly about themselves.
* Alienation, depression.
* Victimized by the past, past lives, etc.
* Spacey.
* Know-it-all who insists on being right and/or attempts domination of others.
* Overly detached and/or dissociated.

Malfunctions: Energetic disorders. Spiritual depression. Rashes. Dementia and/or Alzheimer's disease. Anxiety. Bipolar disorders. Headaches, migraines, strokes, brain tumors, epilepsy, Multiple sclerosis, Parkinson's disease, Attention Deficit Disorder (ADD) and dyslexia, Lou Gehrig's disease, mental illnesses, schizophrenia, multiple personality disorder.

Through the Chakras

Level of relationship:

1st Chakra – Tribal, family.
2nd Chakra – One-on-one.
3rd Chakra – With physical self.
4th Chakra – With self and all others including the Divine.
5th Chakra – To our personal truths.
6th Chakra – To knowledge, wisdom, and vision.
7th Chakra – To our ideal/higher self.

Goals:

1st Chakra – Stability, grounding, physical health, prosperity, trust.
2nd Chakra – Pleasure, healthy sexuality, feeling.
3rd Chakra – Vitality, purpose, strength of will, vitality, spontaneity.
4th Chakra – Stability, trust, physical health, prosperity, grounding.
5th Chakra – Clear communication, creativity, understanding of beliefs.
6th Chakra – Psychic perception, imagination, clear seeing, accurate interpretation.
7th Chakra – Wisdom, knowledge, spiritual connection, consciousness.

Challenges:

1st Chakra – Fear
2nd Chakra – Guilt
3rd Chakra – Shame
4th Chakra – Grief
5th Chakra – Lies
6th Chakra – Illusion
7th Chakra – Attachment

Addictions:

1st Chakra – Food, gambling, shopping, work
2nd Chakra – Alcohol, sex, heroin
3rd Chakra – Amphetamines, cocaine, caffeine, work, anger
4th Chakra – Tobacco (smoking), sugar, love, marijuana
5th Chakra – Opiates, marijuana
6th Chakra – Hallucinogens, marijuana
7th Chakra – Religion, spiritual practices

© Tessa Cason, 2022.

Basic Needs

Your significant-other tells you the two of you have to talk. "Oh no," you think! "He's going to end our relationship. It's over. How can that be? I love him sooooo much! I don't want it to be over! What am I going to do if it is over?" Oh, poor-woe-is-me as the back of your hand lands on your forehead.

Interesting reaction, assuming the worst, the relationship will end. Let's examine this reaction:

One of your basic needs is CONNECTION, TO BELONG, AND ROMANCE. Another basic need is SECURITY.

Both of these basic needs seem to be threatened. She responds with her number one pay-off, self-pity, "Oh, poor woe is me."

When they sit down on the sofa together he says, "We have to talk about what we are doing for the holidays, your family or mine?"

"Whoa," you think a little surprised and embarrassed. "The relationship isn't ending. He's talking about events to come that haven't happened yet!"

Our behavior is governed by our basic needs and our pay-offs for not creating our desired reality.

Let's look more closely at both our basic needs and pay-offs.

OUR BASIC NEEDS...

There are a number of different theories in regards to the Basic Human Needs. For simplicity, this section will cover Tony Robbins' six Basic Needs. Tony believes that to change our lives, we need to understand how the situation meets our six BASIC NEEDS.

The 6 BASIC HUMAN NEEDS are:

NEED #1: CERTAINTY
A need for security, stability, safety, consistency, order, and predictability.

NEED #2: Uncertainty/Variety
A need for adventure, challenges, surprises, and suspense.

© Tessa Cason, 2022.

NEED #3: Accomplishment and Feeling Unique
A need to feel significant and important.
A need of achievement and fulfillment.

NEED #4: Connection
A need to belong, friendships, and a sense of unity,
A need for warmth and romance.

NEED #5: Growth
A need to learn and constantly grow emotionally, intellectually, and spiritually

NEED #6: Contribution
A need to be of service and make a difference.
A need to contribute and give, philanthropy

Even though we each have the same basic needs, they play out differently in our lives.

Some people that crave excitement and suspense in their lives (need #2), might be bored if life was too consistent (need #1). For others, they need stability (need #1). Too much uncertainty (need #2) could create fear and anxiety.

Some people need and want a lot of togetherness (need #4). Without connection, they might feel alone and separate from others. For others, this much togetherness could be stifling and suffocating.

For some, they prefer to "blend in" (need #4). The thought of standing out, being different (need #3) is traumatizing. For those that don't want to be like everyone, that prefer to be an original, the thought of being just like everyone else is too confining and limiting (need #4).

Our needs can play out in positive or negative ways. For example, the need for significance can be accomplished by doing something great or we can make ourselves feel significant by criticizing someone else's accomplishments – same need, different way of achieving it.

Our needs can change throughout our life. Sarah, a childhood friend that I have known for 60+ years, has cycled through a number of the needs at various times in her life. As children, we both were on the swim team and very competitive with each other. Accomplishment was important for both of us (need #3). Her need for achievement continued in high school being president of the debate team, but another need started to emerge. Romance, courtship, love became important (need #4).

"Charles is so dreamy, don't you think?"

"Charlie, my next-door neighbor? You think Charlie is dreamy? He's just a boy like any other boy," I would say. She totally disagreed with me.

© Tessa Cason, 2022.

In college, she began to feel a need to be of service, wanting to make a difference in children's lives (need #6). She became a child psychologist.

After marrying and having three of her own kids, being a stay-at-home mom, being involved in her kid's lives became her main focus (need #4). As their children matured, wanting to be able to pay for their children's college educations, financial security (#1) became a focus.

After the kids left home and they became empty nesters, they decided they wanted to be more adventuresome and do some traveling (need #2). Now I get texts of sunsets from the places they visit.

Our needs will change based on the circumstances of our lives, in the different stages of our lives.

Pay-offs for Not Creating Our Desired Reality

Why would someone not want to create a successful reality? Why would someone not want happiness, peace, fulfillment, and love?

Instead of success and happiness, some are seduced by pain and suffering. In our society, there is a belief, "No pain, no gain." Many people don't change until their back is against the wall, until they've reached "rock bottom," when change becomes a must.

There are "pay-offs" for not creating a successful, prosperous, fulfilling, and joyful reality. Usually, there is one or two that is our go-to pay-off.

Pay-off #1 – Avoidance

We would rather avoid…success, failure, being loved, loving, being alone, being with others, risks, challenges, responsibilities, obligations, fears, hurt, commitment, disappointment, contentment, being seen, being judged, and the list goes on.

Take success, for instant. Think back to all the statements you have heard about success. "It's lonely at the top." "How will you know who your friends are?" "Your "friends," do they want to be with you because of you, the person you are or because of your success and what it would mean for them?"

What about Personal Power? "Power corrupts." "Powerful people are conceited, ruthless, driven, thoughtless, and self-centered." Why would anyone want to be powerful?

"You can't have it all." "Money brings nothing but unhappiness." "Money is the root of all evils." "Will you remember me when you get rich and famous?" "What would I do with the money? I don't know anything about investing. I'm not smart enough to figure it out."

Are you a good steward of money? If you had financial wealth, would you spend it wisely? Would you be responsible and accountable? Is it okay to say "no" to someone in need and less fortunate than yourself? Does saying "no" make you selfish, incite insults that you are thinking of no one but yourself? Do you just avoid the whole scenario?

I had a client, Sam that had inherited $500,000 and became very popular. Six months later, he had less than before he received his inheritance. His bottom line? It was not okay for him to have more than anyone else.

When his new friends asked for something, he would fulfill their wish and/or need. He bought one person a $30,000 car. Another asked for money for a down payment on a house. For another he paid their school tuition. When all the money was gone, so were the friends. When he was evicted from his apartment, the person he gave the down payment to for a house would not even let Sam sleep on the couch!

Sam realized that he gave all his money away and preferred not being wealthy. By giving all his money away, Sam avoided being wealthy and other's thinking he was better than them. Never having money, Sam never learned how to manage money. He found having money attracted those less fortunate to take advantage of his naïveté. He wanted to avoid dealing with people that would take advantage of him. He said his life was easier not having money.

Pay-off #1 is Avoidance. What am I avoiding? What failure am I avoiding? What success am I avoiding? Am I avoiding the responsibility of success? Am I avoiding obligations? Fears? Challenges? Anger?

When we do not feel we have the tools and skills to manage our lives, finances, successes, and/or relationships, we will avoid taking action, making decisions, moving forward in our lives, and/or getting involved in relationships. Avoidance.

Pay-off #2 – Blame

You know the kind…they are always pointing the finger of blame at someone or something else other than themselves. It is never their fault. Never! The words "accountable" and "responsible" are not even in their vocabulary.

How many times have you heard:

* I am the way I am because of my screwed-up parents.
* It's your fault! Not mine.
* I thought you took care of it.
* My boss treats me as if I am worthless.
* My spouse does not want me to do that.

Pay-off #2 – Blame. We blame others for our failures. It is easier to blame others than to take responsibility, to take an honest look at ourselves. There is always someone else or God/Goddess that can be blamed. It is always someone else's fault.

Victim. Hopeless. Helplessness. Powerless. Lack of self-reliance, self-esteem, and self-confidence. Seemingly, without any options. Someone else has the power and control. Someone else is in control of them and their life. Refusal to take responsibility. Not willing to be accountable. Unreliable. Stuck in denial.

Pay-off #3 – Self Pity

"Oh, poor woe is me! No one loves me. No one to help me. I have to do this all by myself. I do everything for them and they do nothing for me! No one cares about me! Nothing ever goes my way. Life has always and will always be a struggle. I never get any breaks in life"…and on and on…

Another victim, everything is hopeless. Their situation is helpless. No one can help them. If someone offered to help, they would refuse with a number of reasons why someone could not help them. Only they can do it right. No one else would be able to figure it out. It is their "responsibility" so they have to do it themselves. If they let someone else help, it would not be done correctly. They would have to redo it so they might as well do it themselves. They turn down any and all help and then feel sorry for themselves that they have to do the work themselves.

Pay-off #3 – Self-pity. Victim. Martyr. Helpless. Life is hopeless.

Pay-off #4 – Guarantee

"Promise me, if I love you, you will never hurt me, abandon me, or reject me. You will marry me, love me forever and ever, and we will live happily ever after. When you do, then I will love you."

Wanting a guarantee is usually a biggie. "Promise me, if I try, I will succeed. I won't fail. I won't look stupid. I will succeed the first time. I will be a hero. Others will admire me."

Many people reach that fork in the path. One would take them to their heart's desire, fulfillment, and contentment. The second path, more traveled, takes them down a path of mediocrity that lacks passion, excitement, and joy but will pay the bills.

If one sets out on the first path, toward their heart's desires and their dreams, if they tried and did not succeed, there would be tremendous pain, disappointment, and embarrassment. Everyone knew they had charted their course and set sail. Everyone knew their intentions and hopes. If they failed, they would look foolish, incompetent, and stupid in the eyes of those that love and admire them.

Or maybe when they reach their goal they will discover the goal did not bring the joy and fulfillment they thought it would. All that work, planning, and sacrificing they would have to do and joy was not the prize. How sad and unhappy they would be. How disillusioned they would feel. So, why even try?

Pain, disappointment, embarrassment, disillusionment, is it really worth the risk? But, with a guarantee that they would accomplish their heart's desire and be a hero, most likely, they would take the first path toward their dreams and heart's desire.

© Tessa Cason, 2022.

Many times, if avoidance (pay-off #1) is a top pay-off, guarantee might be as well.

Pay-off #4 – Guarantee…wanting a promise it will work. We hold out for the guarantee even though we know there are no guarantees. We don't create our reality because we don't have a guarantee.

Pay-off #5 Self-Righteous/Anger

Some people would rather be angry than to be at peace. Somehow, they think there is power in being angry. Being at peace is submissive and weak. If they were nice, they would be used and abused. Vulnerability is a handicap, not a strength!

These are the people that constantly complain. Nothing is ever right. They never direct their comments to someone that has the power to solve and/or resolve their problem. They would rather find fault with what they perceive as not being right. They have all the answers. But no one has ever asked them for the solution.

Anger is their defense. "Life is cruel and harsh. There are no free lunches." Anger is the mechanism they use to push others out of their lives. They don't want anyone to see the true them for fear of rejection. They use their anger as a manipulation to control others. They would rather be sarcastic and cynical than be vulnerable.

Pay-off #5: Self-Righteous/Anger…righteous so to feel hurt and/or angry. Refusal to resolve the hurt and anger. Wanting to feel hurt. Wanting to feel angry. Wanting to have the right to feel angry. This pay-off is about "anger" that they won't do anything about. If they really wanted to let go of the anger, they would do something about it.

Pay-off #6 – Self Importance

These people find their importance in life by being the worst of the worst and/or grander than the best. When you are relating an incident that happened to you, they are the type that have to top your story with a story that is twice as horrendous or magnificent as yours. They have to outdo everything you do, compete with you, even though you were never competing or in competition with them in any way. They have to be better than you by either being the worst of the worst or the grandest of the grand.

In 2000, a woman asked if she paid my way, would I be her roommate on a two week trip to Peru with a spiritual teacher? Soon after departing, I was quick to realize why five of her friends declined the same offer. She had a morphine pump in her spine, feeding her morphine 24-hours a day. With everyone that sat down at her table for a meal, she went into her whole, painful medical history and problems.

© Tessa Cason, 2022.

Picture this: Machu Picchu, sunrise service with a shaman, she has a coughing fit. Does she remove herself from the group, walk away? No. Seven people went to her aid, offering water, cough drops, Reiki, to walk her over to an area where she could sit. She remained in the crowd, refusing any help, all while the shaman is trying to conduct the ceremony.

Pay-off #6 – Self Importance. Better than, worse than. Always a competition. Always proving how important they are. Always wanting the spotlight.

Pay-off #7 – Clinging to the Past

Moving forward in our lives can be frightening, scary, and not at all fun. The unknown of the future can create a great deal of stress within us, particularly if we do not think we have the tools and skills to handle what needs to be accomplished.

Childhood was so much easier when we were daddy's little princess or mom's favorite. We had a roof over our head, food in the refrigerator. We were cared for, financially supported, and loved unconditionally. Then the time came when we had to grow up, leave home, and go out into the big, frightening world, all on our own, as adults.

By clinging to the past we don't have to risk moving forward and failing. We don't have to be courageous, confident, or discerning. We don't have to face challenges or make decisions. We can blame our incompetence on fear instead of an unwillingness to learn new skills. We don't have to be truthful to ourselves about the depth of our character.

Imagine if Thomas Edison, Alexander Bell, Bill Gates, or Steven Jobs clung to the past. There would be no electricity, telephones, Microsoft, or Apple. By clinging to the past, we cheat ourselves of life, new adventures, developing new skills, discovering new facets of ourselves.

Pay-off #7 – Clinging to the Past, fear of moving forward, life will never be as good in the present or future than it was in the past.

What makes certain people cling to their pay-off(s)?

This list could be long. Here are a few reasons that the pay-off might be alluring:

* They don't know how to create the reality they desire.
* They might think this is the best life can be for them.
* They might think they don't have the skills necessary to create the life they desire.
* They might believe being successful could make them a target.
* They might fail if they tried to reach for something outside their reach.
* They don't want to put the energy into something that might not happen.

© Tessa Cason, 2022.

The very things we now wish that we could hold onto and keep safe from change were themselves originally produced by changes. And many of those changes, in their day, looked just as daunting as any in the present do. No matter how solid and comfortable and necessary the status quo feels today, it was once new, untried, and uncomfortable. Change is not only the path ahead, but it is also the path behind us.

        William Bridges

David Hawkins' Map of Consciousness

Levels of Consciousness

[Higher Altitudes]

Enlightenment	700-1000
Peace	600
Joy	540
Love	500
Reason	400
Acceptance	350
Willingness	310
Neutrality	250

[Lower Altitudes]

Courage	200
Pride	175
Anger	150
Desire	125
Fear	100
Grief	75
Apathy	50
Guilt	30
Shame	20

© *David R. Hawkins, Power vs. Force, The Hidden Determinants of Human Behavior, 1995, 1998, 2004, 2012.*

The Map of Consciousness (MOC) is a valuable tool. Our lives can be enhanced when we calibrate the people, teachers, books, learning institutions, health practice, etc on the Map of Consciousness.

The Map was developed by David Hawkins and introduced in his book *Power vs Force: The Hidden Determinant of Human Behavior*. It illustrates and outlines the levels of human consciousness. Twenty years of research involving millions of calibrations on thousands of test subjects of all ages, personality types, and all walks of life went into developing the Map of Consciousness.

With the Map, there is a lower altitude and a higher altitude. When we are in the lower altitudes, we are influenced by that level of consciousness whether that be fear, anger, or courage. Once we are able to maintain Neutrality, 250, we are in control of our lives. Anything less, 249 and lower, the emotion of that level is in charge.

At Neutrality (250), we learn not to take or make everything personal. When we are Willing (310) and Accepting (350), we open up new avenues of well-being.

"Love heals all." The Love at 500 on the Map is the love that heals even though some want to believe it is romantic love that heals (which it is not).

When we are in the higher altitudes, 250 or higher, we are able to objectively evaluate. The lenses through which we see the world has been cleaned.

When developing our intuition, our intuition will be more accurate when we are able to maintain the higher altitudes of 250 or higher. Anything less, when we are in the lower altitudes, our intuition will be "tainted" by the lower level emotions of fear, grief, and/or anger.

© Tessa Cason, 2022.

Mind Chatter – A Valuable Tool!

Mind chatter...that constant stream of thoughts that seem to have little value other than to possibly distract us. Most people think of mind chatter as something negative. I disagree. Mind chatter can be a very valuable tool for growth, healing, and learning about ourselves.

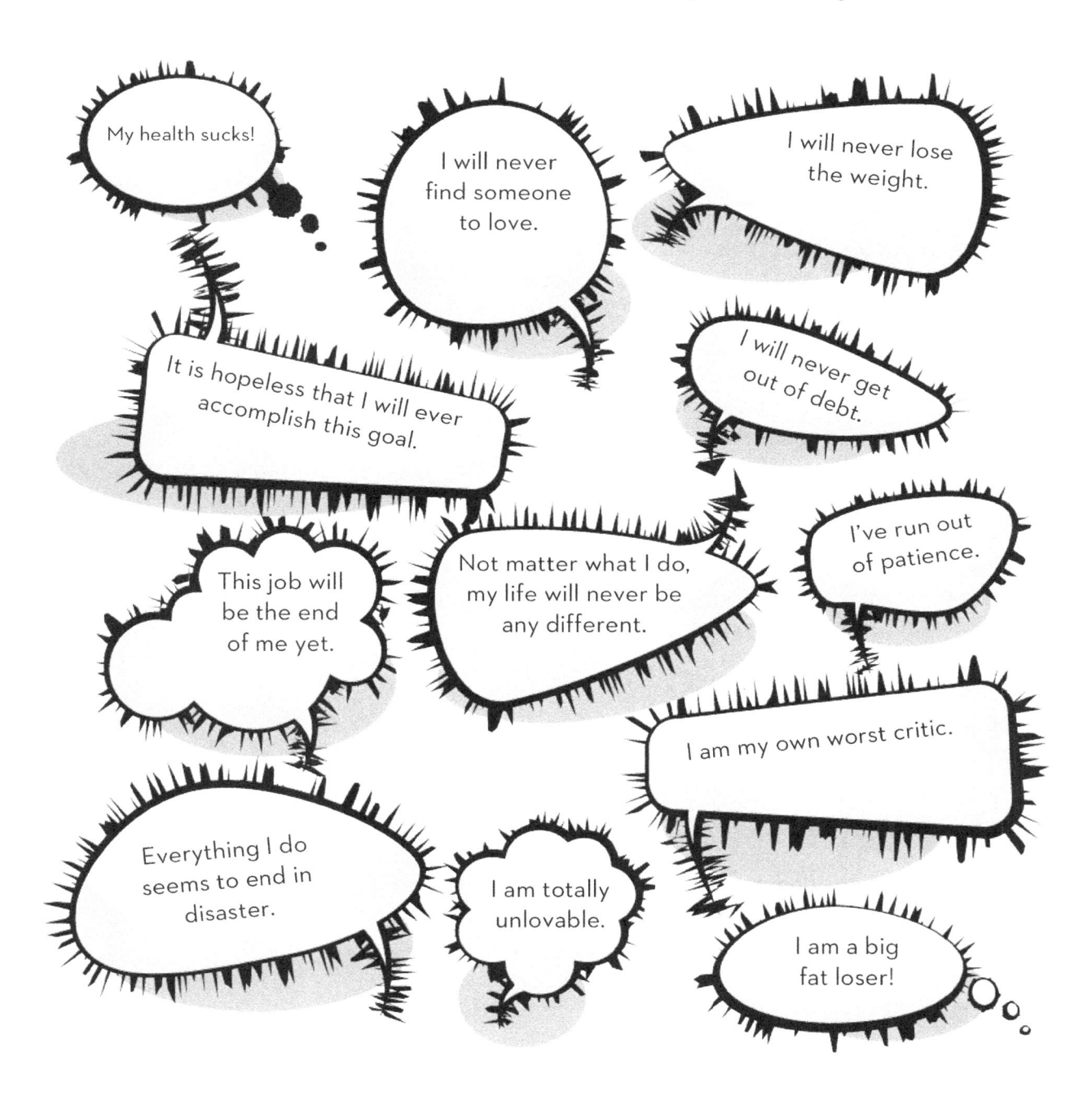

- My health sucks!
- I will never find someone to love.
- I will never lose the weight.
- It is hopeless that I will ever accomplish this goal.
- I will never get out of debt.
- This job will be the end of me yet.
- Not matter what I do, my life will never be any different.
- I've run out of patience.
- I am my own worst critic.
- Everything I do seems to end in disaster.
- I am totally unlovable.
- I am a big fat loser!

© Tessa Cason, 2022.

Does your mind chatter go something like this?

"I will never accomplish this goal."
"I will never find someone to love."
"I will never lose the weight."
"This job will be the end of me yet."
"My health sucks."
"I will never get out of debt."
"I am my own worst critic."
"I've run out of patience."
"Everything I do seems to end in disaster."

If the desire is personal growth, to learn, grow, and thrive, then maybe mind chatter is attempting to point out that which is **preventing us** from learning, growing, and thriving.

"I will never accomplish this goal."
 * Is the issue about hope?
 * The skills and abilities to accomplish the goal?
 * Time management?

"I will never find someone to love."
 * Is this about being vulnerable and the fear of being rejected?
 * Is it easier to say you will never find anyone rather than process your fears and insecurities?

"I will never lose the weight."
 * Weight is only a symptom of dysfunctional beliefs.
 * Are you willing to look at the anger?
 * Do you really want to be vibrant, visible, and present?

"This job will be the end of me yet."
 * Are you willing to put the work into creating your dream job?
 * What can you do to increase your enjoyment of the job you currently have?
 * Do you need additional training to be able to perform your job more effectively?

"My health sucks."
 * Are you willing to change your lifestyle so your health doesn't suck?
 * What is the issue of focusing time, energy, and money on you?
 * If you don't take care of your body, where will you live?

"I will never get out of debt."
 * What have you done to learn about money management?
 * Are you willing to curb your spending?
 * Are you willing to do whatever it takes to get out of debt?

©Tessa Cason, 2022.

"I AM MY OWN WORSE CRITIC."
  * Is this a form of self-punishment?
  * Do you find fault with yourself before anyone else can?
  * Is this a fear of success, prosperity, of moving forward with your life and all the scary things that can happen when you are successful, prosperous, and visible?

"EVERYTHING I DO SEEMS TO END IN DISASTER."
  * Everything? Is this an exaggeration or for real?
  * Does your importance come because everything you do ends in disaster?
  * Is this your identity, the disaster monster?

"I'VE RUN OUT OF PATIENCE."
  * At whom? Yourself? Is this a way to make yourself wrong?
  * Is this a temper tantrum because you aren't getting what you want?
  * Do you have the tools, skills, and abilities to do what you are doing differently to have a different outcome?

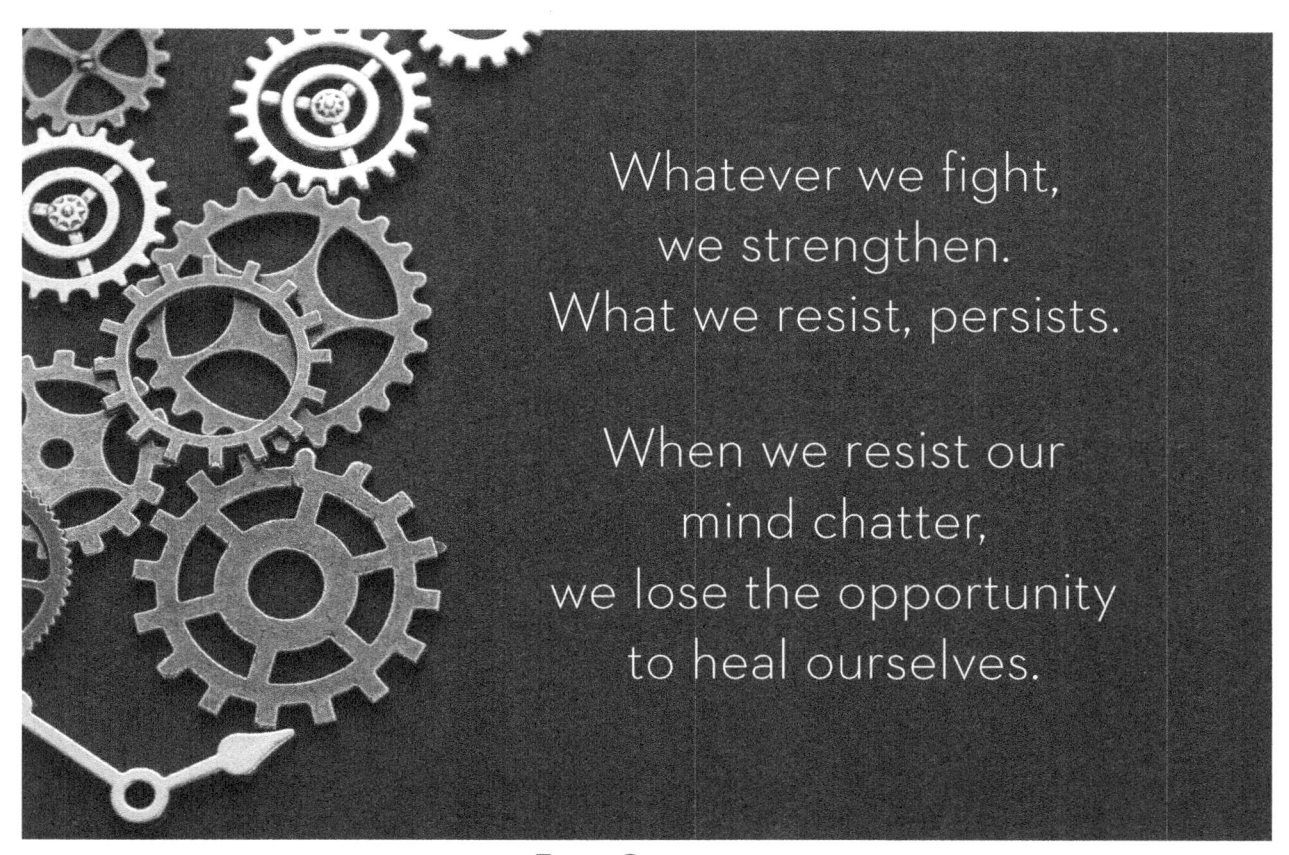

> Whatever we fight, we strengthen.
> What we resist, persists.
>
> When we resist our mind chatter, we lose the opportunity to heal ourselves.

© Tessa Cason, 2022.

Books by Tessa Cason

All Things EFT Tapping Manual

* Why does EFT Tapping work for some and not for others?
* How do you personalize EFT Tapping to be most effective for you?
* What is the very first tapping statement you need to tap?

This manual provides instructions on how to heal our disappointments, regrets, and painful memories.

EFT Tapping information has instructions on what to do if a tapping statement does not clear, what to do if tapping doesn't work for you, and how to write your own tapping statements.

We must eliminate the dysfunctional beliefs if we want to make changes in our lives. EFT Tapping can do just that. EFT Tapping is a simple, yet very powerful tool to heal our beliefs, emotions, painful memories, and stories.

500 EFT Tapping Statements for Moving Out of Survival

Survival is stress on steroids. It's feeling anxious and not good enough. Survival may be the most important topic we can heal within ourselves. Survival is programmed into our DNA.

Ella returned home from the market with her three year old daughter to find a note from her husband that he did not want to be married any longer. Under the note were divorce papers, the number of the divorce attorney, and $500.

Wanting to be able to give her daughter a wonderful childhood, she had to figure out how to survive and thrive. This is her story and the tapping statements she tapped.

Dr. John Montgomery says, "All 'negative,' or distressing, emotions, like fear, disgust, or anxiety, can be thought of as 'survival-mode' emotions: they signal that our survival and well-being may be at risk."

80 EFT Tapping Statements for Change

If it is not okay or safe for our lives to change, every time our lives change, the body is subjected to a tremendous amount of stress.

After graduating from high school, Charlie's dad told Charlie he could continue to live at home, but he would be charged room and board. At 18, Charlie was now financially responsible for himself. He was able to find a job and moved out.

Within a year, circumstances forced Charlie to move back home. Day after day, Charlie rode the bus to work. After work, he rode the bus home. One day as Charlie was riding the bus to work, he noticed another regular rider, Dan, tapping his head.

Together Dan and Charlie began tapping. Find out the results of their tapping and the statements they tapped.

300 EFT Tapping Statements for Self-defeating Behaviors, Victim, Self-pity

Tom had lots of excuses and reasons for his lack of "results." His boss, Robert MacGregor, saw the potential Tom had and asked his longtime friend, Sam Anderson, a life coach, to work with Tom. Read Tom's story to understand how Tom was able to step into his potential.

Self defeating behaviors take us away from our goals, from what we want, leaving us feeling exhausted, disempowered, and defeated. Self defeating thoughts are the negative thoughts we have about ourselves and/or the world around us such as "I'm not good enough", "I have to be perfect to be accepted."

Most likely, you have tried to change the self-defeating and self sabotage behavior, yet here you are with the same patterns.

100 EFT Tapping Statements for Feeling Fulfilled

John wasn't sure what would fulfill him. He loved his job and didn't want to find a new career, but he wasn't feeling fulfilled in his life. With the help of his wife, John found what would be fulfilling.

Fulfillment is a simple formula, actually. It's the follow-through that might be the problem.

What would prevent you from being fulfilled? Do you know what the blocks might be, the reason you remain out of sync, unfulfilled? Is it about leaving your comfort zone or maybe it's that you allow your limitations to define your life?

It is possible to remove the blocks, heal the beliefs on the subconscious level, and move toward your desire for fulfillment. To do so, we need a powerful tool. One such tool is EFT Tapping, the Emotional Freedom Technique.

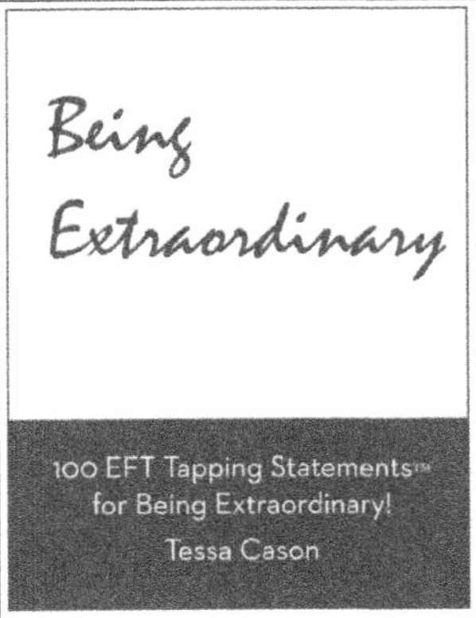

100 EFT Tapping Statements for Being Extraordinary!

Accomplishing extraordinary performances, having incredible successes, or earning large sums of money does not equate to an extraordinary person. This book is about discovering your extraordinary character.

Extraordinary – Exceeding ordinary, beyond ordinary.

Extraordinary starts with the self, our character, depth, and strength of our being. It's being congruent, walking our talk. It is the love, compassion, and tenderness we show ourselves. It's the pure and highest essence of our being.

Rebecca was approaching a time in her life in which she was doing some soul searching and examining her life. She didn't feel extraordinary. In her late 50s, she felt she was just ordinary. She reached out to Tessa. The email exchanges are included in this book along with tapping statements.

400 EFT Tapping Statements for Being Empowered and Successful

Being empowered is not about brute strength or the height of our successes. It is the strength, substance, and character of our inner being. It is knowing that whatever life throws at us, we will prevail.

Ava has just started a business with her two very successful sisters. She wants the business with her sisters to succeed, yet, she doesn't feel empowered. She doesn't want to feel as if the business would fail because of her and is ready to do the emotional work so she matches her sisters' power and success.

Sophie, Ava's roommate and an EFT practitioner-in-training, works with Ava. With Sophie's help, Ava begins to feel empowered and that her business with her sisters will be a success.

300 EFT Tapping Statements for Healing the Self

We live in a complex world with multiple influences. At birth, it starts with our parents and soon afterwards, the influence of other family members (grandparents, siblings, etc.), TV shows, cartoon characters, commercials, and peers. As we get older, we have the influences of teachers, coaches, tutors, television and movie stars, pop stars, sports heroes, and so many other.

When Pete was offered a promotion at work and was not excited about something he had worked so hard to accomplish, he knew he needed to find some answers. He thought he was living his mother's version of his life. He didn't know what brought him joy.

With the help of EFT and an EFT Practitioner, Pete was able to discover his version of his life, what brought him joy, and how to live a fulfilling life.

EFT Tapping for Anxiety, Fear, Anger, Self Pity, Courage (1,000 Tapping Statements)

Anxiety is a combination of 4 things: Unidentified Anger, Hurt, Fear, and Self Pity. We expect error, rejection, humiliation, and actually start to anticipate it.

When we are not in present time, we are either in the past or the future. Anger is the past. Fear is the future. Fear could actually be anger that we failed in the past and most likely will fail again in the future.

It takes courage on our part to heal the anxiety, identify the hurt, and to give up the self-pity. To heal, to thrive, and flourish, we need to address not only the Anxiety, but also the fear, anger, self pity, and hurt.

Healing is not about managing symptoms. It's about alleviating the cause of the symptoms.

80 EFT Tapping Statements for Feeling Less Than and Anxiety

Rene was excited for the year long mentoring program she enrolled in. *How wonderful*, she thought, *to be surrounded with like-minded people.* Five months into the program, she abruptly dropped out. Find out how her feeling Less Than and her Anxiety sabotaged her personal growth.

Anxiety has four parts: unidentified anger, hurt, fear, and self-pity. Living in a state of fear, we want a guarantee that our decisions and choices will produce the results or outcomes that we want. Feeling less than is played out in a cycle of shame, hopelessness, and self-pity. We feel shame about who we are, that we have little value, and that we are not good enough.

Feeling "less than" spirals down into depression, survival, and self-sabotage.

240 EFT Tapping Statements for Fear

Two months before school ended, Lennie was downsized from as a high school music teacher. When he was unable to find another job, fear crept into his thoughts. What if he couldn't find a job in music again? He wasn't qualified to do anything different. He was scared that he would not be able to support his family and they would end up homeless. He could feel the fear as his stomach was in knots.

Fear is that sense of dread, knots in the stomach, chill that runs down our spine, and the inability to breathe. We all know it. Fight-Flight-Freeze.

Fear is a self-protection mechanism. It is an internal alarm system that alerts us to potential harm. When we are in present time, we have the courage, awareness, wisdom, discernment, and confidence to identify and handle that which could cause us harm.

80 EFT Tapping Statements for Anxiety and Worry

"I just can't do this anymore," said Frank to his wife Mary. "You worry about everything. When we got married, your anxiety was something you did every now and then. But now you are paranoid about everything. I leave for work and you act like you are never going to see me again."

Anxiety is a combination of 4 things: unidentified anger, hurt, fear, self-pity. We expect error, rejection, humiliation, and actually start to anticipate it. It is an internal response to a perceived threat to our well-being. We feel threatened by an abstract, unknown danger that could harm us in the future.

Worry is a mild form of anxiety. Worry is a tendency to mull over and over and over anxiety-provoking thoughts. Worry is thinking, in an obsessive way, about something that has happened or will happen. Going over something again and again and asking, "What will I do? What should I have done?"

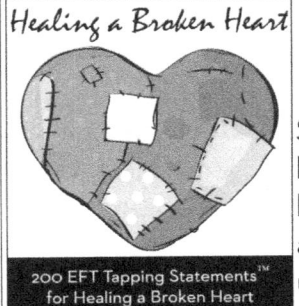

200 ET Tapping Statements for Healing a Broken Heart

She found someone who made her feel cherished, valued, and loved. Tall, dark, and handsome as well as aware, present and understanding. Matt was an awesome guy. He thought she, too, was someone special, intriguing, and awesome.

Matt was promoted at work which meant months away from home and thus, decided to end their relationship. Her best friend introduced her to EFT Tapping to heal her broken heart.

Time does not heal all. Healing the grief of a broken heart is not easy. Grief is more than sadness. Grief is a loss. Something of value is gone. Grief is an intense loss that breaks our hearts.

Over time, unhealed grief becomes anger, blame, resentment, and/or remorse. To heal a broken heart, we need to identify, acknowledge, and healed the dysfunctional beliefs. EFT Tapping can help.

400 EFT Tapping Statements for Dealing with Emotions

Did you see the movie Pleasantville with Tobey Maguire and Reese Witherspoon, two siblings who are trapped in a 1950s black and white TV show, set in a small midwest town where everything is seemingly perfect. David and Jennifer (Tobey and Reese) must pretend they are Bud and Mary Sue Parker, the son and daughter in the TV show.

Slowly, the town begins changing from black and white to color as the townspeople begin to experience emotions. Experiencing emotions is like adding color to a black and white movie. Color adds a depth, enjoyment, and pleasure to the movie. Emotions add depth, enjoyment, and pleasure to our lives.

Emotions add animation, richness, and warmth to our lives. They give our lives meaning and fullness. Without emotions, our lives would be as boring as watching a black and white movie.

80 EFT Tapping Statements for Abandonment

Feelings of abandonment can be triggered by the ending of a relationship as well as the death of an individual. Even though we may have an intellectual understanding of death, there is still a feeling of abandonment when someone we treasure dies. For a small child, they do not understand death. They may still expect the parent to return at any time.

Even though Kevin drove an expensive sports car he wasn't the playboy type. He wanted to settle down and start a family. Kevin felt Susan could be "the one." He wanted to talk to her about taking their relationship to the next level.

Before Kevin could talk to Susan, she ended the relationship because of his insecurities in their relationship. She felt it had to do with the abandonment of his mom when he was a child. This book gives you the exact statements that Kevin tapped to deal with his insecurities in relationships.

EFT Tapping Statements for A Broken Heart: Abandonment, Anger, Depression, Grief, Emotional Healing (1,000 Statements)

Time does not heal all. When our hearts have been shattered, we feel nothing will ever be the same again. We are flooded with emotions... anger, grief, depression...

Regardless of what led to the broken heart, maybe a death, divorce, or a breakup, the result is the same...a broken heart. To heal a broken heart is not only about healing the grief, but also the feelings of abandonment, anger, and depression.

Being abandoned is a verb. It is something that "happens to us." The result of being abandoned is anger, grief, and depression. Grief is the sadness we experience when we have lost something of value.

In order to heal, we need to resolve the anger, grief, abandonment, and depression that resulted from our hearts being fractured.

200 EFT Tapping Statements for Wealth

After graduating from high school, Amy looked for a job for a solid year unsuccessfully! She lacked the necessary experience and education. She felt like she was in a vicious cycle, going round and round and round. Finally, she was hired at a large chain store. For the last eight years, she has been shuffled, unhappily, between different departments.

As a birthday gift, her mom gave her a session with an EFT Practitioner to determine what she wanted to do with her life. Follow along with Amy on her journey to self-discovery.

What we manifest in our lives is a direct result of our beliefs. If we have a mentality of wealth and abundance, we will prosper and thrive.

Our beliefs determine the level of our wealth and abundance. To heal our dysfunctional beliefs, we need a powerful tool. EFT Tapping is one such tool.

EFT Tapping Statements for Prosperity, Survival, Courage, Personal Power, Success
(1,000 Statements)

What we believe determines our prosperity. Our beliefs determine our thoughts and feelings which in turn determine our choices and decisions. Therefore, what we manifest in our lives is a direct result of our beliefs. If we are happy and joyful, we will see happiness in everything. If we are fearful, we will see fear around every corner. If we have a mentality of abundance, we will prosper.

It is difficult to be prosperous when we are stuck in survival. In survival, we feel disempowered to thrive. We can only survive. It takes Courage to step into our Personal Power and to Succeed. We need a powerful tool to heal our dysfunctional beliefs. EFT Tapping is one such tool.

In this book, there are 200 tapping statements for each of these 5 topics - Prosperity, Survival, Courage, Personal Power, and Success.

80 EFT Tapping Statements for Abundance, Wealth, Money

Abby just had her 46th birthday. She tried to celebrate but she didn't have anything to be happy about. Her parents had died in a car accident the Christmas before while driving home from her new home after celebrating Christmas. Both of her parents were real estate agents. She was their transaction coordinator. The three of them had their own offices, handling any real estate transaction that someone might need. Without them, she had no real estate transactions to coordinate.

Abby funds were running dry. She had applied for jobs without success. Abby talked to every one she and her parents knew in hopes of finding a job. With the slow real estate market, she was unable to find any work.

Find out how Abby turned her life around and the exact statements that Abby tapped to deal with her monetary issues.

400 EFT Tapping Statements for Dreams to Reality

Have you done everything you were supposed to do for your dreams to become reality? You were clear on what they were. You made your vision boards with lots of pictures of what you desired. You visualized them coming true and living that life. You've stated your affirmations over and over and over for their fulfillment. You released and allowed the Universe to handle the details. And, now, dust is collecting on your vision boards and you are still waiting for the Universe to handle the details.

Our dreams are our hopes and desires of what we want to come true one day. They are snapshots of what we want our future to be. Yet, sometimes, maybe most of the time, our dreams do not become reality and never manifest themselves in our lives. We gave up on our dreams a long time ago.

Jane shares her story of how she used EFT Tapping to turn her dreams into reality.

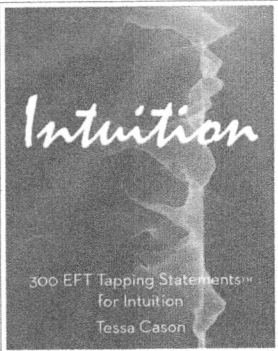

300 EFT Tapping Statements for Intuition

Quinn was one of Tessa's students in her Developing Your Intuition class. She had been hesitant to develop her intuition. One of her basic needs was Belonging. If she was intuitive, she might not belong and thus, realized this was part of her hesitation.

She also had a tendency to avoid which also wasn't conductive to developing her intuition. Tessa wrote out some EFT Tapping statements for her to tap:
* I ignore my inner voice.
* No one I know uses intuition.
* I'm too logical to be intuitive.
* Being intuitive is too complicated.

Included in this book are exercises and helpful hints to develop your intuition as well info on Symbolism, Colors, Number, Charkas, Asking Questions of Our Intuition, Archetypes, and 36 Possible Reasons We Took Physical Form.

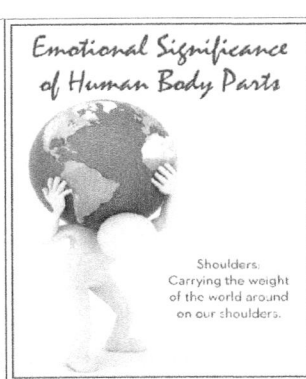

Emotional Significance of Human Body Parts. Chasing the Pain

"We carry the weight of the world around on our shoulders." The emotional significance of the shoulder is about responsibility.

The body "talks" to us...in its language. To understand what the body is saying, we need to learn the body's language.

Jona greeted me at the airport gate on crutches. After hugging each other, she asked what the left ankle meant. I told her the left side of the body had to do with what's going on in the inside and the ankles had to do with commitments.

She had been dating a man for the last two months and he just proposed.

Chasing the Pain is a technique with EFT Tapping that as we tap for a physical pain we are experiencing, the original pain might disappear only to be felt in a different part of the body.

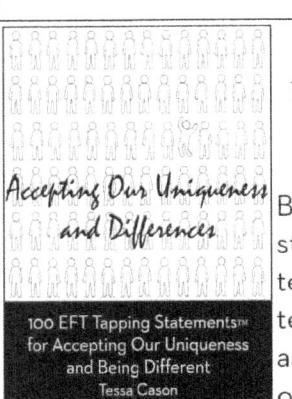

100 EFT Tapping Statements for Accepting Our Uniqueness and Being Different

Brian was an intelligent high school student with average grades. He tested high on all the assessment tests. Brian didn't think of himself as intelligent since his grades were only average. He didn't plan on going to college because he thought he wasn't smart enough and would flunk out.

His counselor knew otherwise and suggested Brian retake the tests to see if the tests were wrong. Find out Brian's scores after he retook the tests and how Mr. Cole introduced EFT Tapping to Brian.

If you were your unique self, do you fear being alone, rejected, or labeled as "undesirable?" Or maybe it's being laughed at and ridiculed for being different and unique?

When we play our lives safe, we end up feeling angry, anxious, powerless, hopeless, and depressed.

Muscle Testing. Obstacles and Helpful Hints

Muscle testing is a method in which we can converse with the subconscious mind as well as the body's nervous system and energy field.

This book details 10 obstacles and 10 helpful hints to successfully muscle test.

One obstacle is that it is a necessity that the tester be someone that calibrates the same, or above, that of the testee, on David Hawkins' Map of Consciousness or be in the higher altitudes, 250 or higher, on the Map.

Helpful hint: When muscle testing, the tester and testee should not make eye contact with each other. With eye contact, the answer would be "our" energy instead of the "testee's" energy.

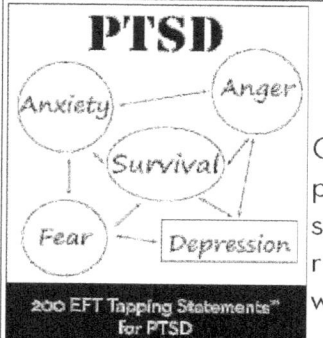

200 EFT Tapping Statements for PTSD

George believed that if he prepared for his death, it was signaling the Universe he was ready to die. George did die without preparing his wife.

George took care of everything. The only thing Helen had to take care of George.

After George died, she had no idea if they owned the home they lived in, if George had life insurance, how to pay bills, if they had money, if they did, where was it? She didn't know if George had left a will. She was not prepared for George's death or how to take care of everything that George took care of.

With the help of friends and EFT Tapping, Helen was able to heal and learn how to take care of everything that George once did.

Healing is not about managing symptoms. It is about alleviating the cause of the symptoms.

EFT Tapping Statements for PTSD, Survival, Disempowered, Fear, Anger (1,200 Statements)

The potential exists for anyone that is in any life threatening situation in which they fear for their life, that believes death is imminent, to experience PTSD.

With PTSD, our Survival is at stake. As a result of our survival being threatened, we feel Disempowered to thrive. We can only survive. When we are caught in Survival, Fear is a prevalent emotion. When we feel Disempowered, Anger is just beneath the surface.

To heal, to thrive, and flourish, we need to address not only the PTSD, but also Survival and Feeling Disempowered, Fear, and Anger. (Thus, the 5 topics in this PTSD Workbook.)

Healing PTSD is a process in which we must desensitize, decrease, and heal the survival response. EFT Tapping is the best method to do so.

200 EFT Tapping Statements for Conflict

"Hi, Julia. So glad you called." Excitedly, I said, "I just finished decorating the house and I'm ready for Christmas!"

Not at all thrilled to be talking to her sister-on-law, Julia said, "That's why I'm calling. You don't mind if I host the family Christmas get-together, do you?"

A little surprised, I said, "Well, I do.

"Tough," she said. "I'm hosting Christmas this year."

This wasn't the first "conflict" with her sister-in-law. But, Audrey was a conflict coward and did not engage.

After EFT Tapping, Audrey overcame her issues with conflict. Find out how and who hosted Christmas that year!

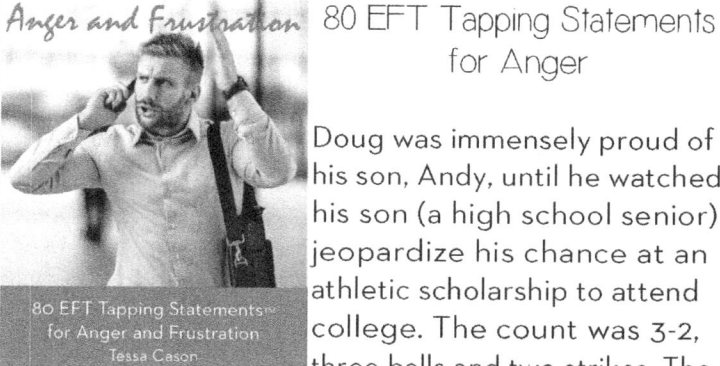

80 EFT Tapping Statements for Anger

Doug was immensely proud of his son, Andy, until he watched his son (a high school senior) jeopardize his chance at an athletic scholarship to attend college. The count was 3-2, three balls and two strikes. The final pitch was thrown and Andy let it go by. The umpire shouts, "Strike!" Andy has just struck out.

"What's wrong with your eyes old man?" Andy shouts at the umpire. "That was a ball. It wasn't in the strike zone. Need instant replay so you can see it in slow motion? I'm not out!"

Andy, was following his father's example of being a rageaholic. EFT Tapping helped both Doug and Andy to take control of his life and his anger.

Anger is not right or wrong, healthy or unhealthy. It is the expression of anger that makes it right or wrong, healthy or unhealthy.

400 ET Tapping Statements for Being a Champion

Jack was a professional runner that injured himself at the US Championships. He was unable to compete at the World Championship. The previous year, Jack had won gold at the World Championships. After six months, he still was not able to run even though the doctors assured him he should be able to run. He had exhausted all medical and physical therapy treatments without success or hope of being able to run pain-free.

Our of frustration, Jack decided to look at the mental piece with a transformation coach. Follow Jack's recovery back to the track through EFT Tapping.

Champions are rare. If being a champion was easy then everyone would be a champion and a champion would not be anything special. It is in the difficulty of the task that, once accomplished, makes a champion great.

EFT Tapping Statements for Champion, Personal Power, Success, Self Confidence, Role Model (1,000 Statements)

Being a champion is more than just being successful. It is the achievement of excellence. It is more than just being competent. It is about stepping into one's power. It is more than just setting goals. It is the achievement of those goals with perseverance, dedication, and determination. It is not just about the practicing, training, and learning. It is the application and implementation of the training and learning into a competition and into everyday situations.

Champions are successful, but not all successful people are champions. Champions are powerful, but not all powerful people are champions. Champions are confident but not all confident people are champions. Champions dream big but not all people that dream big are champions.

300 EFT Tapping Statements for Dealing with Obnoxious People

Three siblings were each dealing with an obnoxious person in their lives. Katherine was dealing with a co-worker that took credit for her accomplishments.

Megan, a professional athlete, was distracted by a narcissistic team member that disrupted practice and thus, her performances at meets.

Peter was a very successful college student that had a Teaching Assistant jealous of everything that Peter was and the TA was not.

Read how each resolved and solved their issue with an obnoxious person.

80 EFT Tapping Statements for Self Esteem

Ron had driven a semi-trailer truck for 30 years for the same company. To celebrate his 60th birthday and 30 years of service, his company had a celebration for him. After the celebration, Ron's boss suggested that he find a job that was more age appropriate. Ron's lack of self-esteem was interfering with moving on with his life. This book gives you the exact statements that Ron tapped to heal his lack of self esteem, self respect, and self-pride.

From birth to about the age of seven, we learn self love from mom. From about the age of seven through twelve, from dad we learn self esteem, earned loved. Self esteem is about the feelings, respect, and pride we have in ourselves.

The lack of self esteem shows up in our lives as a lack self respect and/or pride in ourselves. This "lack" will taint every area of our lives.

340 EFT Tapping Statements for Healing From the Loss of a Loved One

Grief is more than sadness. It is more than unhappiness. Grief is a loss. Something of value is gone. Grief is an intense loss that breaks our heart. Loss can be the death of a loved one, a pet, a way of life, a job, a marriage, one's own imminent death. Grief is real.

Over time, unhealed grief becomes anger, resentment, blame, and/or remorse. We become someone that we are not. It takes courage to move through the grief and all the emotions buried deep within.

John's father died of a heart attack while gardening. A year after his death, John still was not able to move on or be happy. His wife handed him a business card of an EFT Practitioner and recommended therapy to heal the grief. After working with the Practitioner, John was able to find his joy again.

100 EFT Tapping Statements for Feeling Deserving

Sarah, a sophomore in college, was unsure of what to declare as her major. She met with a guidance counselor who wanted to chat first.

Sarah thought of herself as an accident since she had two older siblings who had already moved out of the house when she was five. Her parents had been looking forward to an empty nest, instead, they had a third child that was just starting school.

Sarah had felt undeserving her whole life, even though her parents loved her dearly and never treated her life an accident.

Travel the path Sarah walked with the counselor to finally feel deserving.

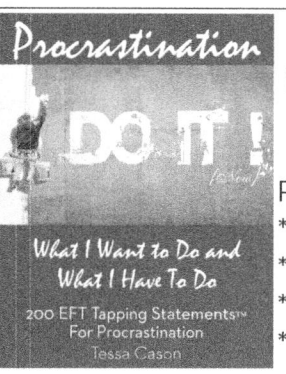

200 EFT Tapping Statements for Procrastination, What I Want to Do and What I Have to Do

Procrastination is about avoiding.
* What are we avoiding?
* What are we afraid to find out?
* What are we not wanting to do?
* What are we not willing to face?

Is it:
* We don't have the tools and skills to do something.
* Rebellion
* Lack of motivation.
* Not knowing what needs to be done.
* Poor time management.

The list is long why we procrastinate and what it could be about. What do we do to heal our procrastination tendencies? EFT Tapping. To heal we have to be able to recognize, acknowledge, and take ownership of that which we want to heal. Then we have to delete the dysfunctional beliefs on the subconscious level. EFT is one such tool that can do just that.

80 EFT Tapping Statements for Relationship with Self

Stephanie, now 55 years old, used to be excited about life and about her life. That was 35 years ago. She was engaged to the love of her life. A month before the wedding her fiancée ran off with a beauty queen.

After 35 years, Stephanie still felt defeated, beaten, defective, broken, and flawed. She was still resentful. She had become comfortable in apathy because she did not know how to move beyond her self-pity.

With the help of EFT Tapping, Stephanie was able to heal her wounded self and begin to live life again.

Do you feel disconnected from yourself? Do you feel as if you could never be whole? Do you feel defeated by life? To change our lives, we have to be able to recognize, acknowledge, and take ownership of that which we want to change. Then heal the dysfunctional beliefs on a subconscious level. EFT Tapping can help.

700 EFT Tapping Statements for Weight, Emotional Eating, & Food Cravings

Emma's sister's wedding was fast approaching. She would be asked at the wedding how her diet was going.

Emma has struggled with her weight for the last 35 years, since high school. Out of desperation, Hannah began working with an EFT Practitioner. Follow her journey to healing the cause of her weight issues.

Excess weight, food cravings, emotional eating, and overeating are symptoms of deeper unresolved issues beneath the weight. Attempting to solve the problem by only dealing with the symptoms is ineffective and does not heal the issue.

Weight is the symptom. The usual programs for weight loss aren't working because they are attempting to solve the problem by dealing with the symptom instead of healing the cause.

EFT Tapping Statements for Weight + Food Cravings, Anger, Grief, Not Good Enough, Failure (1,150 Statements)

Excess weight, food cravings, emotional eating, and overeating are symptoms of deeper issues beneath the weight. Attempting to solve the problem by only dealing with the symptoms is ineffective and does not heal the issue.

The usual programs for weight loss aren't working because they are attempting to solve the problem by dealing with the symptom instead of healing the cause.

IF WE WANT TO HEAL OUR WEIGHT ISSUES, WE NEED TO HEAL THE CAUSE...THE DYSFUNCTIONAL BELIEFS AND EMOTIONS.

HEALING IS NOT ABOUT MANAGING SYMPTOMS. IT'S ABOUT ALLEVIATING THE CAUSE OF THE SYMPTOMS.

80 EFT Tapping Statements for Addictions

Derrick's mom died when he was a senior in high school. His dad (an alcoholic) told Derrick that as soon as he graduated from high school, he was on his own.

The day that Derrick graduated from high school, he went down and enlisted in the army. In the army, he started to drink. A month after his enlistment concluded, he met a wonderful woman. They married and had a child.

One day when Derrick returned home from the bar, he found an empty house and a note. The note told him that since has unwilling to admit he was an alcoholic or to go to counseling, she was left with only one choice. That choice was to relocate herself and their daughter to some place safe, away from him.

Derrick felt he had nothing to live for. He discovered someone at work that was a recovering alcoholic. She introduced her secret, EFT Tapping, to Derrick.

80 EFT Tapping Statements for Weight and Emotional Eating

Excess weight is a symptom, not the cause of overeating and emotional eating.

The day that Tracy was graduating from UCLA, she received a phone call that her father had fallen and had been hospitalized. She was on the next flight home to Dallas. It was decided that her father needed surgery and that Tracy should stay on for a short while to care for her dad. No one asked Tracy what she wanted. But, she stayed anyway.

Seven months later, even though her father had mended, Tracy had become her father's caregiver. This is not what Tracy had planned to do with her life after graduating from college. Every month, over the course of the seven unhappy months, Tracy's weight spiraled up, until she was at her highest weight EVER.

This book gives you the exact statements that Tracy tapped to heal the cause of her weight gain.

80 EFT Tapping Statements for Manifesting a Romantic Relationship

Tanya tells the story about her best friend, Nica. Nica wants a relationship. She wants to be in love, the happily-ever-after kind of love. Nica is self-absorbed, self-centered, smart, and pretty.

Nica has had several long-term relationships but, never allows anyone close enough to get to know her. When she is in between boyfriends, she always whines:

* No man will ever want me.
* The odds are slim to none that I will find anyone.
* I have a bad track record with men so I give up.
* There will never be anyone for me.
* My desires will never be fulfilled.

Tanya is a tapper and finally Nica agrees to do some tapping as a last resort! The Tapping Statements that Nica tapped to manifest a relationship are listed in this eBook.

80 EFT Tapping Statements for Social Anxiety

In social settings, Johnny felt very awkward. He did not enjoy the limelight or any attention focused on him at all!

"Dude," Johnny's buddies would say. "When are you going to get over this fear of talking to a woman?" Johnny would laugh off their comments.

Social Anxiety – Dreading, fearing, and/or expecting to be rejected and/or humiliated by others in social settings.

* A feeling of discomfort, fear, dread, or worry that is centered on our interactions with other people.
* Fear of being judged negatively by others.
* Fear of being evaluated negatively by others.

Is there hope for those that have social anxiety? Yes. EFT Tapping. Tap the statements that Johnny tapped to overcome his social anxiety.

80 EFT Tapping Statements for Adult Children of Alcoholics

Did you have a parent that was an alcoholic? Do you have difficulty relating and connecting to others? Do you have a strong need to be perfect? Is your self-esteem low and judge yourself harshly? Do you have a fear of abandonment and rejection? If so, then EFT Tapping might help.

Rebecca had lost her 4th job. She was defensive, argumentative, and resentful. Rebecca knew her boss was right in firing her.

Rebecca's childhood was anything but idyllic. Her father was a raging alcoholic. She was terrified of his anger. Rebecca tried to be perfect so her dad couldn't find fault with her. Home life was hell. She had to grow up really fast and was never allow to be a kid or to play.

Rebecca did see an EFT Practitioner and was able to heal the anger, the need to be perfect, and other issues one has when they have an alcoholic parent.

200 EFT Tapping Statements for Knowing God

So many questions surround this topic, God. Does God exist or is God a fabrication? Is God for real or just a concept? If God does exist, then what is God's role in our lives?

Do our prayers get answered or are we praying in vain? Does God make mistakes? God created Lucifer and then kicked out a third of his angels from heaven along with Lucifer. Was Lucifer a mistake and all the angels that choose to follow Lucifer? Do we just want to believe that a supreme being really cares about us, gave us our lives' purpose, a mission, and a destiny? God is as varied as there are people.

Many have said that God gave humans the power of choice and free will. If this is true, the consequences of our actions are ours alone. Yet, there are those who believe that God could intervene. God should take action to protect and provide for us.

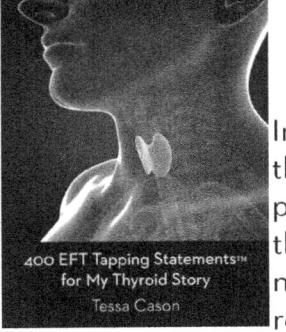

400 ET Tapping Statements for My Thyroid Story

In 2005, I was diagnosed with thyroid cancer. I researched the potential cause and discovered that 20 years after exposure to natural gas, thyroid issues will result. 20 years previous to the diagnosis, I lived in a townhouse for 850 days that had a gas leak.

While pursuing healing modalities after the exposure to natural gas, I began to realize that about 50% of our health issues are emotionally produced. The other 50% are the result of environmental factors such as smoking, chemicals, accidents, and/or hereditary.

I did not believe my emotional issues caused the thyroid cancer. It was the result of an environmental factor outside myself. BUT, since the thyroid was affected, if I worked on the emotional issues that had to do with the thyroid, it should impact the thyroid cancer. That was my theory.

100 EFT Tapping Statements for Fear of Computers

Can you image strapping on your Jet pack to get to work? Traveling on the Hyperloop that travels at speeds up to 600 mph to visit a friend that lives in another state? Stepping into your self-driving car that chauffeurs you to the restaurant? Soon all of these will be a part of our lives.

Modern technology! Most everyone knows that the computer can answer most any question. Most every job today and jobs of the future require at least some knowledge of computers.

Grandmere was intimidated by the computer. Her motivation was her granddaughter would was moving to another country. Granddaughter wants her to learn to use the computer so they can Skype when she is out of the country. Read how Grandmere was able to overcome her anxiety and fear of the computer.

200 EFT Tapping Statements for Sex

Is sex about the act or is sex about the intimacy shared by the act? Is sex about the orgasms or is it about the connection, touching, and cuddling?

In most culture, sex/lovemaking/intercourse is not discussed, explored, or a polite topic of conversation. For a fulfilling and satisfying sexual relationship, communication is important, yet many couples find it difficult to talk about sex.

Can you talk to your partner about sex?
Are you comfortable with your sexuality?
Do you know your partner's sexual strategy?

Our attitude, beliefs, and emotions determine our thoughts and feeling about sex. Dysfunctional beliefs can interfere with a healthy, fulfilling, satisfying sexual relationship. If we want to make changes in our lives, we have to recognize, acknowledge, and take ownership of our dysfunctional beliefs and emotions.

200 EFT Tapping Statements for Positive Thinking vs Positive Avoidance

If we keep piling more Band-Aids over a wound, the wound is still there. At some point, the wound needs to be examined, cleaned, and treated in order for heal.

Sometimes it is just "easier" to think positive when we really don't want to look at an issue. Positive Avoidance is denying the truth of a situation. It is a denial of our experience and our feelings about the situation.

When we try to push down our negative emotions, it is like trying to push a ball underwater. The ball pops back up.

Positive Thinking is the act of thinking good or affirmative thoughts, finding the silver lining around a dark cloud, and looking on the more favorable side of an event or condition. It is not denial, avoidance, or false optimism.

Books and Kindles eBooks by Tessa Cason

80 EFT Tapping Statements for:
Abandonment
Abundance, Wealth, Money
Addictions
Adult Children of Alcoholics
Anger and Frustration
Anxiety and Worry
Change
"Less Than" and Anxiety
Manifesting a Romantic Relationship
Relationship with Self
Self Esteem
Social Anxiety
Weight and Emotional Eating

100 EFT Tapping Statements for Accepting Our Uniqueness and Being Different
100 EFT Tapping Statements for Being Extraordinary!
100 EFT Tapping Statements for Fear of Computers
100 EFT Tapping Statements for Feeling Deserving
100 EFT Tapping Statements for Feeling Fulfilled
200 EFT Tapping Statements for Conflict
200 EFT Tapping Statements for Healing a Broken Heart
200 EFT Tapping Statements for Knowing God
200 EFT Tapping Statements for Positive Thinking vs Positive Avoidance
200 EFT Tapping Statements for Procrastination
200 EFT Tapping Statements for PTSD
200 EFT Tapping Statements for Sex
200 EFT Tapping Statements for Wealth
240 EFT Tapping Statements for Fear
300 EFT Tapping Statements for Healing the Self
300 EFT Tapping Statements for Dealing with Obnoxious People
300 EFT Tapping Statements for Intuition
300 EFT Tapping Statements for Self-defeating Behaviors, Victim, Self-pity
340 EFT Tapping Statements for Healing From the Loss of a Loved One
400 EFT Tapping Statements for Being a Champion
400 EFT Tapping Statements for Being Empowered and Successful
400 EFT Tapping Statements for Dealing with Emotions
400 EFT Tapping Statements for Dreams to Reality
400 EFT Tapping Statements for My Thyroid Story

500 EFT Tapping Statements for Moving Out of Survival
700 EFT Tapping Statements for Weight, Emotional Eating, and Food Cravings
All Things EFT Tapping Manual
Emotional Significance of Human Body Parts
Muscle Testing – Obstacles and Helpful Hints

EFT Tapping Statements for:
A Broken Heart, Abandonment, Anger, Depression, Grief, Emotional Healing
Anxiety, Fear, Anger, Self Pity, Change
Champion, Success, Personal Power, Self Confidence, Leader/Role Model
Prosperity, Survival, Courage, Personal Power, Success
PTSD, Disempowered, Survival, Fear, Anger
Weight & Food Cravings, Anger, Grief, Not Good Enough, Failure

Other Books
Why we Crave What We Crave: The Archetypes of Food Cravings
How to Heal Our Food Cravings

EFT Workbook and Journal for Everyone:
Abandonment
Abundance, Money, Prosperity
Addictions
Adult Children of Alcoholics
Anger, Apathy, Guilt
Anxiety/Worry
Being A Man
Being, Doing, Belonging
Champion
Change
Conflict
Courage
Dark Forces
Decision Making
Depression
Difficult/Toxic Parents
Difficult/Toxic People
Emotional Healing

Fear
Forgiveness
God
Grief
Happiness/Joy
Intuition
Leadership
Live Your Dreams
Life Purpose/Mission
People Pleaser
Perfectionism
Personal Power
Relationship w/Others
Relationship w/Self & Commitment to Self
Self Confidence
Self Worth/Esteem
Sex
Shame
Stress
Success
Survival
Transitions
Trust/Discernment
Victim, Self-pity, Self-Defeating Behavior, Shadow Self
Weight and Emotional Eating

Made in the USA
Monee, IL
19 September 2022